First World War
and Army of Occupation
War Diary
France, Belgium and Germany

17 DIVISION
Divisional Troops
Royal Army Veterinary Corps
29 Mobile Veterinary Section
15 July 1915 - 31 January 1919

WO95/1997/3

The Naval & Military Press Ltd
www.nmarchive.com
Published in association with The National Archives

Published by

The Naval & Military Press Ltd

Unit 10 Ridgewood Industrial Park,

Uckfield, East Sussex,

TN22 5QE England

Tel: +44 (0) 1825 749494

www.naval-military-press.com

www.nmarchive.com

This diary has been reprinted in facsimile from the original. Any imperfections are inevitably reproduced and the quality may fall short of modern type and cartographic standards.

© **Crown Copyright**
Images reproduced by permission of The National Archives, London, England, 2015.

Contents

Document type	Place/Title	Date From	Date To
Heading	WO95/1997/3		
Heading	17th Division Troops 29th Mobile Vety Section Jly 1915- Mar 1919		
Heading	17th Division 29th Mobile Vety Sect. Vol. I 17-31-7-15		
War Diary	Southampton	15/07/1915	15/07/1915
War Diary	Havre	16/07/1915	16/07/1915
War Diary	Lumbres	17/07/1915	18/07/1915
War Diary	Renescure	19/07/1915	19/07/1915
War Diary	Steenvoorde	20/07/1915	24/07/1915
War Diary	Reninghelst	25/07/1915	31/07/1915
Heading	17th Division 29th Mobile Vety Section Vol II August 15		
War Diary	Reninghelst	01/08/1915	31/08/1915
Heading	17th Division 29th Mobile Vet. Sect. Vol 3 Sept 15		
War Diary	Reninghelst	01/09/1915	30/09/1915
Heading	17th Division 29th Mobile Vet. Sect. Vol 4 Oct 15		
War Diary	Reninghelst.	01/10/1915	05/10/1915
War Diary	Reninghelst And Godewaersvelde	06/10/1915	06/10/1915
War Diary	Godewaersvelde	06/10/1915	11/10/1915
War Diary	Steenwoorde	11/10/1915	23/10/1915
War Diary	Steenwoorde	24/10/1915	24/10/1915
War Diary	Poperinghe	24/10/1915	31/10/1915
Heading	17th Division 29th Inf. Ver. Sect. Vol 5 Nov. 15		
War Diary	Poperinghe	01/11/1915	30/11/1915
Heading	17th Div 29th Sub. Ver. Sect. Vol 6		
War Diary	Poperinghe	01/12/1915	31/12/1915
Heading	29th Mobile Vet Section 17th Division Vol VII		
Miscellaneous	Adjutant General		
War Diary	Poperinghe	01/01/1916	08/01/1916
War Diary	Poperinghe Steenwoorde	08/01/1916	08/01/1916
War Diary	Steenwoorde Tilques.	09/01/1916	09/01/1916
War Diary	Tilques	09/01/1916	31/01/1916
Heading	29th Ver. Sect Vol.8		
War Diary	Tilques	01/02/1916	06/02/1916
War Diary	Noir-Carme	06/02/1916	11/02/1916
War Diary	Bussycheure Steenwoorde	12/02/1916	12/02/1916
War Diary	Steenwoorde to Reninghelst	13/02/1916	13/02/1916
War Diary	Reninghelst.	14/02/1916	29/02/1916
Heading	17 29 M. Vet S Vol 9		
War Diary	Reninghelst.	01/03/1916	12/03/1916
War Diary	Caestre	13/03/1916	21/03/1916
War Diary	Caestre Nieppe	22/03/1916	22/03/1916
War Diary	Nieppe	23/03/1916	18/05/1916
War Diary	Nieppe La Motte	19/03/1916	19/03/1916
War Diary	La Motte-Tilques	20/05/1916	20/05/1916
War Diary	Tilques	21/05/1916	12/06/1916
War Diary	Tilques St. Omer Allonville	12/06/1916	12/06/1916
War Diary	Allonville	13/06/1916	27/06/1916
War Diary	Allonville Mericourt	28/06/1916	28/06/1916
War Diary	Mericourt	29/06/1916	30/06/1916

Heading	War Diary 29 Mol. Vet Section 17th Div July 1/31st 1916 17 July 29 M.V.S. Vol 13		
War Diary	Mericourt	01/07/1916	03/07/1916
War Diary	Mericourt-Ribemont	04/07/1916	04/07/1916
War Diary	Ribemont	04/07/1916	10/07/1916
War Diary	Ribemont Cavillon	11/07/1916	11/07/1916
War Diary	Cavillon	12/07/1916	14/07/1916
War Diary	Cavillon-Pont-Remy	15/07/1916	15/07/1916
War Diary	Pont Remy	16/07/1916	22/07/1916
War Diary	Ribemont	22/07/1916	21/08/1916
War Diary	Ribemont Bonnay	21/08/1916	21/08/1916
War Diary	Bonnay Rainneville	22/08/1916	22/08/1916
War Diary	Rainneville Occoches	23/08/1916	23/08/1916
War Diary	Occoches Grincourt	24/08/1916	24/08/1916
War Diary	Grincourt	25/08/1916	31/08/1916
Heading	War Diary Of 29th Mob Vet Section Sept 1916		
War Diary	Grincourt	01/09/1916	21/09/1916
War Diary	Grincourt Le Meillard	22/09/1916	22/09/1916
War Diary	Le Meillard St. Ricquier	23/09/1916	23/09/1916
War Diary	St. Ricquier	24/09/1916	30/09/1916
Heading	War Diary 29 Mobile Vet Section October 1916		
War Diary	St Ricquier	01/10/1916	05/10/1916
War Diary	St Ricquier Conteville	06/10/1916	06/10/1916
War Diary	Conteville Mezerolle	07/10/1916	07/10/1916
War Diary	Mezerolle	08/10/1916	08/10/1916
War Diary	Mezerolle Pas	09/10/1916	09/10/1916
War Diary	Pas Grincourt	10/10/1916	10/10/1916
War Diary	Grincourt	11/10/1916	22/10/1916
War Diary	Treux	23/10/1916	26/10/1916
War Diary	Treux Meaulte	27/10/1916	27/10/1916
War Diary	Meaulte	28/10/1916	30/10/1916
War Diary	Meaulte	31/10/1916	31/10/1916
War Diary	Minden Post	01/11/1916	03/11/1916
War Diary	Mansell Copse	04/11/1916	15/11/1916
War Diary	Daours-Oissy	16/11/1916	16/11/1916
War Diary	Oissy	17/11/1916	31/12/1916
War Diary	Minden Post	01/01/1917	16/01/1917
War Diary	Minden Post Corbie	16/01/1917	16/01/1917
War Diary	Corbie	17/01/1917	31/01/1917
War Diary	Minden-Post	01/02/1917	20/02/1917
War Diary	Heilly	21/02/1917	21/02/1917
War Diary	Le Cauroy.	01/04/1917	08/04/1917
War Diary	Berneville	08/04/1917	12/04/1917
War Diary	Arras	12/04/1917	13/04/1917
War Diary	Agnez-Les Duisans	13/04/1917	25/04/1917
War Diary	Le Cauroy	25/04/1917	01/05/1917
War Diary	Hermaville	02/05/1917	02/05/1917
War Diary	Laresset	12/05/1917	12/05/1917
War Diary	Laresset St Nicholas	12/05/1917	12/05/1917
War Diary	St Nicholas	12/05/1917	31/05/1917
War Diary	Couterelle	31/05/1917	22/06/1917
War Diary	Couturelle Anzin	22/06/1917	30/06/1917
War Diary	Anzin	22/06/1917	15/09/1917
War Diary	Arras	16/09/1917	25/09/1917
War Diary	Arras Lecauroy	25/09/1917	25/09/1917
War Diary	Lecauroy	25/09/1917	04/10/1917

War Diary	Le Cauroy Proven	04/10/1917	05/10/1917
War Diary	Proven	05/10/1917	11/10/1917
War Diary	Ondank	11/10/1917	05/12/1917
War Diary	Proven	05/12/1917	07/12/1917
War Diary	Esquel Becq	07/12/1917	07/12/1917
War Diary	Zutkerque	08/12/1917	13/12/1917
War Diary	Eperlecque	12/12/1917	13/12/1917
War Diary	St. Omer-Baupome	14/12/1917	15/12/1917
War Diary	Achiet Le Petit	14/12/1917	23/12/1917
War Diary	Haplincourt	23/12/1917	21/03/1918
War Diary	Beaulencourt Le Sars	21/03/1918	23/03/1918
War Diary	Le Sars La Boiselle Henencourt	24/03/1918	24/03/1918
War Diary	Henencourt Contay	25/03/1918	25/03/1918
War Diary	Contay Acheux Puchevillers	26/03/1918	26/03/1918
War Diary	Puchevillers Val de Maison	27/03/1918	27/03/1918
War Diary	Val de Maison	28/03/1918	28/03/1918
War Diary	Val de Maison Mirvaux	29/03/1918	29/03/1918
War Diary	Mirvaux	30/03/1918	04/04/1918
War Diary	Flesselles	04/04/1918	11/04/1918
War Diary	Puchevillers	11/04/1918	20/04/1918
War Diary	Arqueves	20/04/1918	23/06/1918
War Diary	Herissart	23/06/1918	08/08/1918
War Diary	Herissart Blancy-Tronville	08/08/1918	08/08/1918
War Diary	Blangy-Tronville Daours	09/08/1918	10/08/1918
War Diary	Daours	10/08/1918	13/08/1918
War Diary	Fouilloy	13/08/1918	18/08/1918
War Diary	Fouilloy Herrisart	18/08/1918	18/08/1918
War Diary	Herrisart	18/08/1918	23/08/1918
War Diary	Herrisart Acheux	24/08/1918	24/08/1918
War Diary	Acheux Englebelmer	24/08/1918	27/08/1918
War Diary	Englebelmer Aveluy	27/08/1918	30/08/1918
War Diary	Aueluy Martinpuich	30/08/1918	30/08/1918
War Diary	Martinpuich	30/08/1918	02/09/1918
War Diary	Martinpuich Beaulencourt	02/09/1918	02/09/1918
War Diary	Beaulencourt	02/09/1918	17/09/1918
War Diary	Lechelle	17/09/1918	05/10/1918
War Diary	Lechelle Fins	05/10/1918	05/10/1918
War Diary	Fins	05/10/1918	08/10/1918
War Diary	Fins Walincourt	08/10/1918	08/10/1918
War Diary	Walincourt Montigny	09/10/1918	09/10/1918
War Diary	Montigny	09/10/1918	23/10/1918
War Diary	Montigny Inchy	23/10/1918	23/10/1918
War Diary	Inchy	23/10/1918	27/10/1918
War Diary	Inchy-Neuvilly	27/10/1918	27/10/1918
War Diary	Neuvilly	27/10/1918	05/11/1918
War Diary	Neuvilly Poix du Nord	05/11/1918	05/11/1918
War Diary	Poix du Nord	06/11/1918	07/11/1918
War Diary	Poix du Nord Locquignol	07/11/1918	07/11/1918
War Diary	Locquignol Tete Noir	08/11/1918	08/11/1918
War Diary	Tete Noir Aulnoye	09/11/1918	09/11/1918
War Diary	Aulnoye	09/11/1918	12/11/1918
War Diary	Aulnoyes Vendegie au Bois	12/11/1918	12/11/1918
War Diary	Vendegies Au Bois Inchy	13/11/1918	13/11/1918
War Diary	Inchy	13/11/1918	08/12/1918
War Diary	Inchy to Masnieres	08/12/1918	08/12/1918
War Diary	Masnieres Hermies	08/12/1919	09/12/1919

War Diary	Hermies Favreuil	09/12/1918	10/12/1918
War Diary	Favreuil to Albert	10/12/1918	11/12/1918
War Diary	Albert & Querrieu	11/12/1918	12/12/1918
War Diary	Querrieu Picquigny	12/12/1918	13/12/1918
War Diary	Picquigny Hallencourt	13/12/1918	14/12/1918
War Diary	Hallencourt	14/12/1918	19/12/1918
War Diary	Cocqueril	19/12/1918	31/01/1919

W095/1997(3)

17TH DIVISION TROOPS

29TH MOBILE VETY SECTION

JLY 1915 - ~~FEB 1919~~ MAR 1919

157/6250

Mjr Dunoon.

29th Mobile Vet.y Sect:

Vol. I

14 – 31-4-15

Page 1

WAR DIARY

J R TINDLE Capt. A.V.C. Army Form C. 2118

INTELLIGENCE SUMMARY C.C. No 29 Mobile Veterinary Section

(Erase heading not required.)

Place	Date	Hour	Summary of Events and Information	Remarks and references to Appendices
SOUTHAMPTON	15/7/15	10.30 A.M.	Arrived at docks	
		12.30 P.M.	Embarked on the transport BLACKWELL	
		4.30	Sailed	
		6 P.M.	1 A.C.C. and twelve men formed a guard for the life-boats.	
HAVRE	16/7/15	2 A.M.	Arrived at Havre.	
		7.30 A.M.	Received orders to report at Point 3 Gare de Mercandise at 6.30 P.M.	
		8 A.M.	Men, horses and vehicles disembarked	
		5 P.M.	1 A.C.C. and six men proceed to Gare de Mercandise report to supply officer	
		5.30 P.M.	Marched to Point 3 Gare de Mercandise	
		6.30 P.M.	Reported to R.T.O.	
		7 P.M.	Horses + vehicles loaded on train	
		10.30 P.M.	Train started	
LUMBRES	17/7/15	8 P.M.	Men, horses and vehicles unloaded	

Army Form C. 2118

WAR DIARY
or
INTELLIGENCE SUMMARY
(Erase heading not required.)

Instructions regarding War Diaries and Intelligence Summaries are contained in F.S. Regs., Part II. and the Staff Manual respectively. Title Pages will be prepared in manuscript.

Place	Date	Hour	Summary of Events and Information	Remarks and references to Appendices
LUMBRES	17.9.15	9.30 P.M.	Men and horses billeted.	
	18.9.15	9 A.M.	Marched to the starting point – Cross roads at Setques (Map HAZEBROUCK)	5-A
		10.30 A.M.	Marched with divisional headquarters to RENESCURE	
RENESCURE		1 P.M.	Arrived at RENESCURE. Men horses billeted	
	19.7.15	9 A.M.	Marched to the starting point EBBLINGHEM station	
		10 A.M.	Marched with divisional headquarters to STEEVOORDE	
STEENVOORDE		2 P.M.	Arrived STEENVOORDE Men and horses billeted	
	20.7.15		Remained in billets	
	21.9.15		Remained in billets. One horse admitted. Eight horse cast	
	22.9.15		Remained in billets. Eight horse admitted. Seven (sick horses in charge of an A.C.C. and 1 man were entrained at CAESTRE and sent out to No 10 Veterinary Hospital	

Army Form C. 2118

WAR DIARY
or
INTELLIGENCE SUMMARY

(Erase heading not required.)

Instructions regarding War Diaries and Intelligence Summaries are contained in F. S. Regs., Part II and the Staff Manual respectively. Title Pages will be prepared in manuscript.

Place	Date	Hour	Summary of Events and Information	Remarks and references to Appendices
STEENVOORDE	23.7.15		Remained in billets. Seven horses admitted	
	24.7.15	1 PM	One horse admitted. Thirteen horses evacuated to CAESTRE for No 10 Veterinary Hospital	
		2 PM	Moved from STEENVOORDE to RENINGHELST. Billeted in a farm on the left of the BOESCHEPPE road (H.2.a)	
RENINGHELST		PM 6.30	Arrived at farm. One horse died	
	25.7.15		2 horses admitted	
	26.7.15		2 horses admitted	
	27.7.15		10 horses admitted	
	28.7.15		1 horse & 1 mule admitted	
	29.7.15		12 horses and 2 mules admitted	
	30.7.15			
	31.7.15		2 horses admitted	

131/6753

17th Kwain

29th Mobile Vet.y Section
Vol II

August 15

Page - 4.

WAR DIARY or INTELLIGENCE SUMMARY

Army Form C. 2118

of J.P.P. Keppel Lieut. a.v.o
O.C. 29th Mobile Veterinary Section

(Erase heading not required.)

Place	Date	Hour	Summary of Events and Information	Remarks and references to Appendices
ENING HELST	1-8-15		(a) Two horses and one mule admitted. One N.C.O. and one man proceed to STEENVOORDE for a horse suffering from debility but found animal had died.	
"	2-8-15		5 Horses admitted into sick lines. One horse died from Pneumonia	
"	3-8-15		5 Horses admitted into sick lines. O.C. and 16 men to GODEWARSVELDE Station to entrain 15 horses and 1 mule to No.10 Veterinary Hospital. One N.C.O. and two men conducted horses. One N.C.O. and Interpreter to TERDEGHEN for horse left there by the Cyclist Co of the 17th Division.	
"	4-8-15		2 Horses admitted to sick lines. O.C. and Interpreter with two men to FLETRE for 2 horses from "B" battery 80th Brigade R.F.A.	
"	5-8-15		3 horses 1 mule to sick lines admitted.	
"	6-8-15		3 horses admitted to sick lines	
"	7-8-15		(b) 2 Horses admitted into sick lines. O.C. 1 N.C.O. and 8 men to GODEWARSVELDE Station with 8 horses and 1 mule leaving 18 horses at station all entrained for No.10 Veterinary Hospital. 1 N.C.O. and 3 men conducting party.	

WAR DIARY or INTELLIGENCE SUMMARY

Army Form C. 2118

Instructions regarding War Diaries and Intelligence Summaries are contained in F. S. Regs., Part II. and the Staff Manual respectively. Title Pages will be prepared in manuscript.

(Erase heading not required.)

Place	Date	Hour	Summary of Events and Information	Remarks and references to Appendices
ENINGHELST	8.8.15.		2 horses and 2 mules admitted to sick lines. C.O. and Interpreter and 1 horse to BOESCHEPE for horse from B battery 80th Brigade R.F.A.	
"	9.8.15.		1 horse admitted to sick lines. C.O. Interpreter, Shoeing Smith and 4 men proceeded to HONDEGHEM for 5 horses.	
"	10.8.15		1 Horse admitted to sick lines. 1 horse and 1 mule discharged from sick lines.	
"	11.8.15		1 Horse and two mules admitted to sick lines. 1 Horse and 1 mule discharged.	
"	12.8.15		4 Horses and 1 mule admitted into sick lines. 1 Horse died. 1 horse destroyed. 1 horse discharged.	
"	13.8.15.		4 Horses and 1 mule admitted to sick lines.	
"	14.8.15		1 Horse admitted into sick lines. 1 N.C.O. and 8 men to GODEWAERSVELDE Station with 4 horses and 4 mules to No.10 Veterinary Hospital. 1 N.C.O. and 1 men as convoy escort & 9 party.	
"	15.8.15		1 Horse admitted to sick lines	

Army Form C. 2118

WAR DIARY
or
INTELLIGENCE SUMMARY
(Erase heading not required.)

Instructions regarding War Diaries and Intelligence Summaries are contained in F. S. Regs., Part II. and the Staff Manual respectively. Title Pages will be prepared in manuscript.

Place	Date	Hour	Summary of Events and Information	Remarks and references to Appendices
WINCHELSEA	16.8.15		1 horse admitted to sick lines	
"	17.8.15		2 horses admitted to sick lines	
"	18.8.15		7 horses and 1 mule to sick lines	
"	19.8.15		2 horses admitted to sick lines	
"	20.8.15		1 horse admitted to sick lines	
"	21.8.15		4 horses and 1 mule to sick lines. 2 N.C.O's and 12 men to ODEWAERSVELDE Station with 10 horses and 3 mules & into and for N10 Veterinary Hospital. 1 N.C.O and 2 men in charge party. 1 horse dis charged from sector	
"	22.8.15		1 horse admitted to sick line	
"	23.8.15		2 horses destroyed.	
"	24.8.15		1 horse admitted to sick line.	
"	25.8.15		4 horses admitted to sick lines	
"	26.8.15		O.C. 2 N.C.O's and 12 men to POPERINGHE Station with 3 cart horses, 9 sick horses and 1 mule entrained to N0 10 Veterinary Hospital. 1 N.C.O and 2 men conducting party. 6 horses and 1 mule admitted to sick lines.	

… … **A.D.S. 29th Div.** Army Form C.2118

WAR DIARY
or
INTELLIGENCE SUMMARY
(Erase heading not required.)

Place	Date	Hour	Summary of Events and Information	Remarks and references to Appendices
ENING.HELST	27/8/18		4 horses admitted to sick lines. 1 horse discharged from Section. LIEUT. J.G. KEPPEL A.V.C took over command of 29th Mobile Veterinary Section in relief of CAPT. R. TINDLE posted ad. V.S. 6th Division.	
"	28/8/18		3 horses admitted to sick lines.	
"	29/8/18		3 horses admitted to sick lines.	
"	30/8/18		4 horses and 4 mules admitted to section as evacuees. 11 horses and 2 mules (of which 1 horse and 2 mules were admitted from formations) were admitted to section. 1 horse and 1 mule admitted to section.	
"	31/8/18		3 horses and 2 mules admitted to section. C.O.'s 2 N.C.O's and 7 men to GODEWAERSVELDE Station with 7 horses and 1 mule entrained to No.10 Veterinary Hospital. 1 N.C.O and 1 man conducting party. 1 horse discharged from section. 4 (of the evacuees) horses handed over to 17th N. mvo ward train.	

2/7016

17th Division

29th Inftie ret: dec:

tot 3

Sept. 15.

September 1915 — Army Form C. 2118

Page 2

999 Kirkel hurtage
O.C. 29th F.A. Vet dept

WAR DIARY
INTELLIGENCE SUMMARY
(Erase heading not required.)

Place	Date	Hour	Summary of Events and Information	Remarks and references to Appendices

ENINGHELST

SEPT 1

Six horses and one mule admitted to section sick lines as follows:—

1. Yorkshire Dragoons. Both were suffering from an injury to near hind coronet and Discharged Cured 13.9.15
2. Queen's Own Oxfordshire Hussars. a bay gelding suffering from Colic. This animal was on the Strenth not having been at command. Colic near the section lines. *Discharged Cured 5.9.15.
3. 7th East Yorks, Bay gelding suffering from Strangles Evacuated 3.9.15.
4. 17th Div Ammunition Column. Mule black gelding suffering from Gunshot wound - sharpnel wound through to Spleen N rad Evacuated 3.9.15
5. 17th Div Ammunition Column. Bay mare in foal. Evacuated 3.9.15.
6. 8th Brigade C.Battery R.F.A. Bay gelding hurt off hind hock - Contusion Evacuated 9.9.15
7. Canadian Divl Royal Engineers Bay gelding suffering from Kick off elbow. Discharged Cured 20.9.15.

Two horses discharged as unfit from the sick lines.
1. Transit Transit Belgian Force a grey gelding hurt Spirit Off fore
2. 52nd Field Ambulance heavy draught horse.

1.9% 99 Kerkel...

WAR DIARY / INTELLIGENCE SUMMARY

Army Form C. 2118
Page 9

Place	Date	Hour	Summary of Events and Information	Remarks and references to Appendices
ENINGHELST	Sept. 2nd		Four horses admitted to section:-	
			1. 79th Brigade R.F.A. Bay horse suffering from Debility. Evacuated 3.9.15	
			2. 12th Manchesters Bay gelding suffering from Crease. Evacuated 3.9.15	
			3. Artillery Mounted Brigade 17th Division H.Q. Brown gelding with contused wound near fore knee. Evacuated 3.9.15	
			4. 52nd Field Ambulance Chestnut horse with contused wound off hind. Evacuated 11.9.15.	
"	3rd		Two horses admitted to sick lines:-	
			1. 77th Co. Royal Engineers Brown gelding with open shot fetlock. Evacuated 7.9.15	
			2. 77th Co. Royal Engineers Bay gelding with Pneumonia. Evacuated 7.9.15	
			O.C. two N.C.O's and fourteen men proceeded to GODEWAERSVELDE to entrain 12 horses and 4 × 4 horses to No.10 Veterinary Hospital NEUFCHATEL. One N.C.O with three men acted as conducting party. Private Taylor horse fell and threw its rider on returning to section. Reported at M.E. DES. C.A.T.S. with slight contused wound was admitted.	
"	4th		Nothing of note. Section routine.	

J.P. Marshall Lt.

WAR DIARY

INTELLIGENCE SUMMARY

(Erase heading not required.)

Army Form C. 2118

page 10

Place	Date	Hour	Summary of Events and Information	Remarks and references to Appendices
ENINGHELST.	SEPT 5th		Two horses admitted to section :-	
			1. Sgt Brigade R.F.A. B battery. Bay gelding with ring bone sore fore and was evacuated on the 7th September.	
			2. 17th Signal Co. Run here with Kit - wound healed and was discharged cured on the 20.9.15.	
			One horse discharged :- Bueno Own Oxfordshire Hussars.	
"	6th		Two horses and one mule admitted to section :-	
			1. 78th Brigade. R.F.A. Brown gelding with Lumbars haemorrhage in an advanced state and very weak with stiffness in hocks and was kept on diet, was treated with fit & gave on 15.9.15	
			2. 79th Brigade. R.F.A. C battery. Bay gelding with strangles and was evacuated on 7.9.16.	
"	7th		Five horses and one mule admitted to section :-	
			1. 17th Div Ammunition Column. Brown horse suspected mange annual kept in isolation and evacuated 7.9.15 to tube to itself. Form No. K.f. 1689	
			2. 17th Div Train No. 2. Co. Bay gelding with Arthritis off hind hock and was discharged cured 13.9.15.	
			3. 17th Div Train No. 2. Co. Bay gelding Ring bone near ft - Evacuated 11.9.15	
			4. 12th Manchester Regt. Bay gelding brittle insensibility - Evacuated 11.9.15. Manual	

WAR DIARY
INTELLIGENCE SUMMARY
(Erase heading not required.)

Army Form C. 2118

Page 1

Place	Date	Hour	Summary of Events and Information	Remarks and references to Appendices
ENINGHELST	SEPT 7th		5. 10th Sherwood Foresters Bayonet wd enlarged fellows near face and alveolus. Evacuated 11.9.15.	
			6. East Yorks Regt. (9th). Bullet grazing forearm febrile the result of animal falling into a trench. Evacuated 11.9.15.	
			O.C. the N.C.O.'s and ten men proceed to RODEWAERSVELDE Station with 8 knees and 3 men to entrain for No. 10 Veteran'y Hospital. 1 N.C.O. and 3 men acted as conducting party. Two knees and three horses admitted into Section.	
8th			1. 7th Lincoln Regt. Bay grazing wd punctured area ft. face and two evacuated 15.9.15.	
			2. 7th Lincoln Regt. Black grazing hole not injury to sen that forward fascia. Evacuated 11.9.15.	
			3. 7th East York Regt. Black grazing wd injury to carriage of forearm one. Evacuated 11.9.15.	
"			4. York Lancs Regt. Bay have here wth shrapnel ten pre ext Evacuated 11.9.16.	
			5. York Lancs Regt. Bay grazing hole wth shrapnel sen his/for and Evacuated 11.9.16	
			One knee and one horse discharged from detain dut here.	39 Retained.

Army Form C. 2118

WAR DIARY

INTELLIGENCE SUMMARY

page 12.

(Erase heading not required.)

Instructions regarding War Diaries and Intelligence Summaries are contained in F. S. Regs., Part II. and the Staff Manual respectively. Title Pages will be prepared in manuscript.

Place	Date	Hour	Summary of Events and Information	Remarks and references to Appendices
RENINGHELST	Sept 8th		1) 9th West Riding Regt - mule	
"	9th		2) H.Q. 17th Division - Chestnut gelding. Four horses and one mule admitted to Section.	
			1) 'C' Bty 85th Brig. R.F.A - Black gelding with a tear-pointed Radius and was destroyed 10.9.15.	
			2) 79th Brig. R.F.A Ammunition Col. Black gelding mule with injury to near hock and Evacuated to No 10 Veterinary Hospital 11.9.15.	
			3) 78th Co. R.E. Chestnut mare with kicked wound off hind foot and Evacuated 11.9.15.	
			4) 2 Co. A.S.C 17th Div Train. Brown mare with Divies near hind and Evacuated No10 Vet. Hospital 11.9.15.	
			5) South Staffs Regt (8th) Brown gelding fair sore near fore and discharged cured 22.9.15.	

1875 Wt. W593/826 1,000,000 4/15 J.B.C. & A. A.D.S.S./Forms/C. 2118.

WAR DIARY
INTELLIGENCE SUMMARY

Page 13

Army Form C. 2118

Place	Date	Hour	Summary of Events and Information	Remarks and references to Appendices
RENINGHELST	Sept 10th		One horse admitted to section. B. Bty 79th Brig. R.F.A. Brown geld. punctured sole off hind and evacuated No.10 Vet Hospital 11.9.15. No.67565 Dr. Wilson A/C trans fever temp 103°/8 hot, wet sheet. One horse and one mule admitted to section.	
"	11th		1. 57th Field Ambulance Black geld - mule not beyond character. Off grazier - strained hound and evacuated hence 15.9.15. 2. North ampton Skins Yeomanry. Bay geld with injury off hock. This animal was collected by O.C.'s animal Capt. BOESCHEPE from Madame DESIRÉ DECANTRE. The horse was left on July 22. 1915. as to whom cases did not give it the animal despite repeated efforts. A Receipt Note was left with to whom the animal appointed by C.O. Evacuated to No.10 Vet Hospital 25.9.15	

Army Form C. 2118

WAR DIARY

INTELLIGENCE SUMMARY

(Erase heading not required.)

page 14

Place	Date	Hour	Summary of Events and Information	Remarks and references to Appendices
ENINGHELST	Sept 11		O.C. 2 N.C.O's and 14 men to GODEWAERSVELDE station to entrain 9 sick horses and 6 mules for No.10 Veterinary Hospital. 1 N.C.O with 2 men conducting party.	
"	12th		Six horses and one mule admitted to section.	
			1) Amm Column 80th Brig R.F.A Chestnut gelding. Cast by Remount officer. Evacuated 15.9.15 to No. 10 Vet. Hospital	Fate returned
			2) Amm Column 80th Brig R.F.A Brown gelding - Cast by Remount officer - "worn out". Evacuated to No.10 Vet Hospital 15.9.15.	
			3) 7th East Yorks Regt. Brown horse - mule. Bone Spavin offhind. Evacuated to No 10 Vet Hospital 15.9.15.	
			4 H.Q. 50th Infantry Brig. Black gelding knee - Sidonitis both fore. Evacuated N o. 70 Vet Hospital 15.9.15.	

WAR DIARY

~~INTELLIGENCE SUMMARY~~ Page 15.

Army Form C. 2118

Place	Date	Hour	Summary of Events and Information	Remarks and references to Appendices
ENINGHELST	Sept 12		5). 10th Lancs Fusiliers Regt. Bay ged. Colnut itching and evacuated to No 0.10 vet Hospital. 15.9.15.	
			6) 9th West Riding Regt. Blackhorse, Quitor near hind evacuated to No 10 vet Hospital 15.9.15.	
			Four horses that she keeps admitted to section.	
"	13.		1) 78th Brig. R.F.A. Chestnut gelding cut Splint near fore and evacuated 15.9.15.	
			2) 28th Brig. R.F.A. Brown gelding injury to top jaw and is in our treatment has knocked get cured 29.9.15	
			3) Yorkshire Dragoons. Bay gelding cut shown near hind and evacuated 16.9.15.	
			4) 17th Legal Co. Chestnut gelding with desmonitis and evacuated	
	15.9.15			

Army Form C. 2118

page 16

WAR DIARY

~~INTELLIGENCE SUMMARY~~

(Erase heading not required.)

Instructions regarding War Diaries and Intelligence Summaries are contained in F. S. Regs, Part II. and the Staff Manual respectively. Title Pages will be prepared in manuscript.

Place	Date	Hour	Summary of Events and Information	Remarks and references to Appendices
DENNGHELST	Sept 13.		Three horses cast shoes got from reserve horses	
			1) No. 2 C.C.S. 17th Div Train.	
			2) Yorkshire Dragoons.	
			3) A. Battery 89th Bgde. R.A.	
"	14		Two horses cast shoes cast from section	
			1) 52 Field Ambulance	
			2) C.Bty 80th Bgde R.A.	
"	15		Ten horses attached to section	
			1) 147 Co. A.S.C. Bay gelding with Deshevr. Evacuated 15.9.15	
			2) 147 Co. A.S.C. Bay gelding with shivering. Evacuated 15.9.15.	
			3) 7th East Yorks Regt.	
			Bay Mare with Lameness. Evacuated 20.9.15	
			4) 7th East Yorks Regt.	
			Worn gelding shivering. Evacuated 25.9.15.	

WAR DIARY

Page 17.

Army Form C. 2118

Instructions regarding War Diaries and Intelligence Summaries are contained in F. S. Regs., Part II. and the Staff Manual respectively. Title Pages will be prepared in manuscript.

(Erase heading not required.)

Place	Date	Hour	Summary of Events and Information	Remarks and references to Appendices
BINGHURST	Sept 15		One horse checked & cured from kicking.	
			1. Bttn. 81 Brigade F.A.	
			O.O. 2.R.C.S. and 9 men to OSEWALEVER DE SHAKIN with 9 horses and to proceed to entrain for NO.10 VETERINARY HOSPITAL NEUFCHATEL 1.N.C.O. and 2 men as conducting party.	
16			2 horses on a 3 mile service to lecture.	
			1) Ammo Col 50th Brigade F.A. Bay gelding interstices	
			2) 3rd Sec 17 Div Ammo Col. Black geld mule interstice Bones Evacuated 20.9.15	
			3) 3rd Sec 17 Div Ammo Col Black geld mule interstice Bones Evacuated 20.9.15 Blackthorn mule Chest by Ramrod Officer for Vice Evacuated 20.9.15	
			4) 3rd Sect. 17 Div Ammo Col. Bay have mule Contusion fat ---- Evacuated 20.9.15	
			5) 149. Co. A.S.C. Bay have mule Strain Curneco on a men Evacuated 20.9.15	

WAR DIARY

INTELLIGENCE SUMMARY

Page 18.

Place	Date	Hour	Summary of Events and Information	Remarks and references to Appendices
PENINGHELST	Sept 16.		Location of Section moved from Point H.2.A BOESCHEPE Road to C.31.d. Point 52. Map 28. A farm house and surroundings were unsuitable for the Section in view of the approaching winter, the new farm buildings good accommodation for the men and shelter in the form of lean to" for the horses do not as providing room for stores, harness forage &c.	
"	17.		The horses admitted to Section:- 1) No.2. Sect 17th D.A.C. Chestnut mare withdrawn off fore and evacuated 20.9.15. 2) Army Col 80th Brig R.F.A. Grey mare not broken to harness and evacuated 20.9.15. One toe chestnut gd. Cured from be chien - gt not - unshod on a hindleg.	

WAR DIARY
INTELLIGENCE SUMMARY

Page 19.

Army Form C. 2118

Place	Date	Hour	Summary of Events and Information	Remarks and references to Appendices
ENINGHELST	Sept 18.		Lieut Lewis admitted to Section.—	
			1.) B. Bty. 78th Brigade. R.A. Chestnut gelding cast inspected mange and evacuated	
			20.9.15.	
			2.) Ammn Col. 78th Brigade. R.A. Brown gelding cast Leaward pelvis evacuated 20.9.15.	
			3.) Ammn Col. 78th Brigade. R.A. Brown mare with open tempore harness sore. This horse was turned in to Section three days ago recovery now despaired of. inca 28.9.15.	
			4.) C.Bty. 80th Brigade R.A. Bay geld. cast fractured scapula evacuated 20.9.15.	
			5.) C.Bty. 80th Brigade R.A. Brown mare not attaining rise in section.	
			6.) C. Bty. 80th Brigade R.A. Bay mare cast Inspected mange evacuated 20.9.15. —	
	19.		Lieut Lewis returned to Section duties:—	
			7) 53 Field Ambulance Black geld. cast by Remount Officer for Broken hand evacuated 20.9.15.	

WAR DIARY

INTELLIGENCE SUMMARY

Army Form C. 2118

Page 20.

Place	Date	Hour	Summary of Events and Information	Remarks and references to Appendices
ENINGHELST	Sept. 19.		2) 53. Field Ambulance. Brown geld. with contused wound off fore. Evacuated 20.9.15.	
			3) B. bty 81 Brigade R.F.A. Brown gelding with contused wound off fore. Evacuated 20.9.15.	
			4) B. bty 81 Brigade R.F.A. Brown geld. with Inguinal hernia. Evacuated 25.9.15.	
			5) 1. Co. A.S.C. attached C. Bty 80 Brigade R.F.A. Inguinal influenza. Evacuated 20.9.15.	
	20		1. 6th Dorset Regt. Bay geld with Splint, always to lameness	
			2) Ammn Col. 79 Brigade R.F.A. Brown mule with Rheumatism admitted to veterinary evacuated 25.9.15.	
			3) C. bty 81 Brigade R.F.A. Bay geld with torn eyelid and sundry treatment	
			1) Horse brass checked from section as cured.	
			2) 17th Signal Co.	
			3) Commanding R.E.	
			4) C. bty 81 Brigade R.F.A.	

Army Form C. 2118

WAR DIARY

~~INTELLIGENCE SUMMARY~~ Page 21.

(Erase heading not required.)

Place	Date	Hour	Summary of Events and Information	Remarks and references to Appendices
RENINGHELST.	Sept. 20		O.C. 2 N.C.O.'s and 9 men proceeded to GODEWAERSVELDE station to return 13 horses and 3 mules to N° 1 VETERINARY HOSPITAL. NEUFCHATEL. ("NOO") and 3 mgr. as conducting party.	
"	21		Four horses admitted to section:- 1) 17th Div. Amm. Col. Bay geld. with splintered shin and very lame and treated in section while fit to travel. Evacuated 25.9.15. 2) Hd. 78th Brigade. S.A. Brown mare with shoulder sinapses evacuated 25.9.15. 3) A. Bay 78th Brigade S.A. Bad mare with sinapses of knee. Evacuated 25.9.15. 4) A bty 80th Brigade S.A. Brown mare with sidebone. Near hind. Evacuated 25.9.15. 5) 93 Co. R.E. Bay geld with wound front off near hind. Evacuated 25.9.15.	
"	22		Three horses admitted to section :- 1) B. Bty. 81 Brigade. Brown geld. with lacerated wound inside thigh and had loss of hair. Animal was brought to section pussing from heavy draught Vessels Vessels were ligated and torn parts brought together with 10 sutures. Animal got cast in on the hoist on the hoists. — See evacuation 29.9.16 2) 10th Sherwood Foresters Regt. Bay geld with intestinal and discharged Anus. 29.9.15.	

WAR DIARY
INTELLIGENCE SUMMARY
Page 22.

(Erase heading not required.)

Army Form C. 2118

Place	Date	Hour	Summary of Events and Information	Remarks and references to Appendices
PENINSULA REST	Sept. 22		3) H.Q. 80th Brigade F.A. Brigade with a considerable number sore. Evacuated 5.9.15.	
"	23.		N.C.O and man who were on conducting party to last horse returned with a quantity of Veterinary Stores for the H.Q's officer's inspection.	
			1) Armr. Col. 80th Brigade F.A. Regt horse with abscess off Shoulder. A very large abscess was present but pus was too shallow and opened. Evacuated 25.9.15.	
			2) Armr. Col. 30th Brigade F.A. Brown mule with contused knee off fore iris in use Treatment.	
			3) 5 Field Ambulance.	
			Brown mule, chronic abscess on Shoulder	
			4) Armr. Col. 79 Brigade F.A. Bayart horse with Arthritis. Animal was very poor and a few days before admission to section had slipped a pinnace from Gaworsky 25.9.15.	
			5) Armr. Col. 79 Brigade F.A. Bay geld mule with neck evil and was destroyed. Evacuated 25.9.15.	
			6) One knee shacker got no cure from Section.	
			1) 1 bay 87 Brigade F.A.	
			Two horses admitted to Section :-	
			1) Yorkshire D registered Black geld. horse puncture of foot - observation was averaged 24.9.15	

WAR DIARY

INTELLIGENCE SUMMARY

Army Form C. 2118

Page 23.

Place	Date	Hour	Summary of Events and Information	Remarks and references to Appendices
RENINGHELST	Sept 25		2) 146. Co. A.S.C. 17 Air Line. Bay horse not picked up well. Evacuated 25.9.15.	
"	26		15 horses and 1 mule evacuated from GODEWAERSVELDE station for No. 10 VETERINARY HOSPITAL NEUFCHATEL. O.C. 2 N.C.O's and 11 men proceeded from section with same. One off: N.C.O. and 3 of the men have since returned from section with the very sick and blind horses. One horse Chestnut Gld. Cross from Sutton :— B. Coy 80th Brigade. G.S. limber proceed POPERINGHE to hut entrain 9 horses returning with Veterinary Stores for V.O's of 4th Division. Two horses and one mule admitted :— 1) 3.Sec. 17 Div Amm. Col. Bay horse not cured eye. Evacuated 29.9.15. 2) B. Bat.y 81 Brigade F.A. Black gld. not laminitis and evacuated 29.9.15. 3) 6th Dorset Regt. Brown mule not injured withers Evacuated 29.9.15.	
"	27		One horse admitted to section :— D. Bat.y 80 Brigade Brown geld. lost shoes n/s hind off fore too in the hindment	

Army Form C. 2118

Page 24.

WAR DIARY

~~INTELLIGENCE SUMMARY~~
(Erase heading not required.)

Instructions regarding War Diaries and Intelligence Summaries are contained in F. S. Regs., Part II. and the Staff Manual respectively. Title Pages will be prepared in manuscript.

Place	Date	Hour	Summary of Events and Information	Remarks and references to Appendices
NINGHELST.	Sept. 28.		One Horse and one Mule admitted to Section.	
			1) B. Bttry 81. Brigade F.A. Horse's gas not delivery wounds 29.9.18.	
			2) No 2 Sec. M. Div Amm Col.	
			I N.C.O. and groom proceeded to YPRES to act as a fatigue party by case dug horse and used as loading them on shotguns lent to the section by the O.C. 17. N in Amm. Column. Horse and Mule being required to take duties for fortnance in view of forthcoming winter.	
	29		Two horses admitted to Section.	
			1) Amm Col. 80 Brigade R.A. Bay horse not Chronic no under treatment	
			2) 10th West Yorks Regt. Brown gave out Sustained haemorrhage in on Section	
			Four horses discharged cured:—	
			1) 78th Brigade R.P.A.	
			2) Amm Col. 76 Brigade R.A.	
			3) 10th Sherwood Foresters Regt.	
			O.C. 2 N.C.O.S and seven proceeded to GODEWAERSVELDE to take 3 horses and 2 mules down to VETERINARY HOSPITAL, NEUFCHATEL. N.C.O and	
			1 man acting as conducting party.	
	30.		One horse admitted to Section:—	
			a Bay 80 Brigade F.A. Brown Horse not Delivered on is in Section.	

1375 W₁. W593/826 1,000,000 4/15 J.B.C. & A. A.D.S.S./Forms/C. 2118.

12/7517

17th Kurram

29th mobile Vet. Sec:
Vol: 4
Oct 15

Page 25

Army Form C. 2118

WAR DIARY
or
INTELLIGENCE SUMMARY
(Erase heading not required.)

O.C. 29. MOBILE VETERINARY SECTION

Place	Date	Hour	Summary of Events and Information	Remarks and references to Appendices
OUTTER RENINGHELST	Oct. 1.	—	5 Horses 1 mule admitted to Section. 1/16 Co. A.S.C. Horse suffering with a wound that developed into a bruise and Evacuated 3-10-15. 149 Co. A.S.C. Br. geld. with splints and Evacuated 3-10-15. 149 Co. A.S.C. Bay geld. Injury to his spine and Evacuated 3-10-15. 77 Co. R.E. Black geld. with injury to Jugular Vein the result of animal being stabbed. Dressed in Section and Evacuated 3-10-15. 9th West Riding Regt. Br. geld. mule with Catarrh and Strains and Evacuated 3-10-15. 17 Signal Co. Grey geld. with frained knees off fore. and Evacuated 3-10-15.	
	Oct. 2.		Two Animals admitted to Section and 1 also charged horses 1 Co. and driven with pain (horses and hind country cart proceeded to DICKEBUSH for 400 feet of timber for Stabling purposes	J.R.KING Lt. O.C. 29 Mob. Vet. Sec.

WAR DIARY or INTELLIGENCE SUMMARY

Army Form C. 2118

Page 26.

Place	Date	Hour	Summary of Events and Information	Remarks and references to Appendices
ENINGHELST	Oct 2	—	Admitted:—	
			78 Bde. R.F.A. Ammunition Column.	
			Bay gelding suffering from a sprain off fore – evacuated 3/10/15.	
			D Bty. 81 Bde. R.F.A.	
			Brown mare with a fractured jaw and evacuated 3-10-15.	
			Two charged Cases.	
			57 F.D. Field Ambulance.	
			Brown mare lame.	
			1 horse and 2 mules admitted to Section.	
"	3.		1 Sect. 17 Div. Amm. Col.	
			Brown gelding lame with a pricked up near off hind and evacuated 5-10-15.	
			1 Sect. 17 Div. Amm. Col.	
			Brown gelding with Sprain near fore evacuated 5-10-15.	
			1 Sect 17 Div. Amm. Col.	
			Brown mare lame with Tetanus, soon after admission cannot was destroyed with intensive spasms of long duration and was destroyed 4-10-15.	
			A.C./N.C.O. and others proceeded to GODEWAERSVELDE Station to escort horses to NO. 10. VETERINARY HOSPITAL.	

Army Form C. 2118

WAR DIARY
or
INTELLIGENCE SUMMARY
(Erase heading not required.)

27.

Place	Date	Hour	Summary of Events and Information	Remarks and references to Appendices
			Continued	
RENINGHELST	Oct 3	-	NEUFCHATEL. I.M.E.O and 1 man as Conducting party	
"	4	-	30 Horses and 2 mules admitted to Section -	
			3rd Bty. 7th Regt. BELGIAN Artillery.	
			1) Chestnut horse with a severe Eye. evacuated 5-10-15.	
			2) Bay horse with wound contused near hind. evacuated 5-10-15	
			3) Black gelding severe wound Perineum. evacuated 5-10-15.	
			4) Bay gelding wound contused hear elbow evacuated 5-10-15	
			5) Bay horse Splint near fore. suppurating Corn both fore and evacuated 5-10-15.	
			C. Bty. 80 Bde. R.F.A.	
			6) Bay gelding punctured behind near fore foot. evacuated 5-10-15.	
			7) Black gelding with an "Avon Shot" fetlock. evacuated 5-10-15	
			8) Black horse with slight injury. evacuated 5-10-15.	
			C. Bty. 81 Bde. R.F.A.	
			9) Bay horse with punctured horses off fore foot — Discharged Cured 7-10-15	7-10-15

WAR DIARY or INTELLIGENCE SUMMARY

PAGE 28.

Army Form C. 2118

Place	Date	Hour	Summary of Events and Information	Remarks and references to Appendices
RENINGHELST	Oct. 4		Continued.	

9) D. Bty. 80 Bde. R.F.A.
10) Chestnut gd. with a Snider off hind evacuated 5-10-15.
11) A. Bty. 78 Bde. R.F.A.
    Bay mare with ulcer open joint and was destroyed same day.
12) Chestnut gelding with Catarrh and evacuated for Dilbery 5-10-15
13) Bay mare with foal.
    Both were evacuated 5-10-15

9) West Riding Regt.
14) Black mare mule with Sprain of tendon Shoulder muscles evacuated 5-10-15.

Lancashire Fusiliers.
15) Bay gelding with discharging wound evacuated 5-10-15.

146. Co. A.S.C.
16) Black gelding with his hoof coming off fore.
17) Bay gelding with colic anuinus had history of severe abdominal pains for the previous 10 days evacuated 5-10-15.
18) Bay mare with Lymma thrck near fore thro char gd. knee 7-10-15.
19) Bay gelding with injury to off hip evacuated 5-10-15.

WAR DIARY
or
INTELLIGENCE SUMMARY
(Erase heading not required.)

Army Form C. 2118

29.   29

Place	Date	Hour	Summary of Events and Information	Remarks and references to Appendices
ENINGHURST.	Oct. 4.		Continued	
			147 Co A.S.C.	
			20) Chestnut mare but Side Bone and Ringbone - generated 5-10-15.	
			21) Bay geld. Tendo above - generated 5-10-15.	
			22) Bay mare. Debility - generated 5-10-15.	
			Commanding R.E.	
			23) Black geld. Ringbone - discharged. Cured 5-10-15.	
			1st MANCHESTERS.	
			(24) Br. geld mule hit Kick wound on near knee - generated 5-10-15.	
			78 Co. R.E.	
			25) Bay geld. hit Kick off fore fetlock - wound - generated 5-10-15.	
			26) Bay geld. hit Suppurating corn off fore - generated 5-10-15.	
			93 Co. R.E.	
			27) Black mare. Contused wound near thigh - generated 5-10-15.	
			17 SIGNAL CO.	
			(28) Blues geld. Suffering with Collar galls - generated 5-10-15.	
			B. Bty. 51st Bde. R.F.A.	
			(29) Roan geld. Injury off hock - generated 5-10-15.	

WAR DIARY or INTELLIGENCE SUMMARY

Army Form C. 2118

Place	Date	Hour	Summary of Events and Information	Remarks and references to Appendices
ENINGHELST	Oct 4	—	Continued. (30) B. have with a contract horses 1 ff hind reverted 3-10-15. (31) B. gets Contracter face reversed 5-10-15. A. Bty. 80 Bde R.F.A. (32) Blact have Withing lane reversed 3-10-15. 3 Sect. 17. Div. Amm. Col. (33) Bay have hose left Spanio Sedans 1 ff for revered 5-10-15. 8 horses and 6 heros admitted to Section. 2 horses discharged as cured from Section. 28 horses and 3 huros and 1 hero left for evacuated to No. 10. VETERINARY. HOSPITAL. NEUFCHATEL. O.C. 2 N.C.O's and 13 men proceeded to GODEWAERSVELDE. Station lentrain animals. 1 N.C.O 3 men acted as conducting party.	
	5		Admissions — 1. Sec. 17 Div. Amm. Col. 1) Blast mare with laminitis reversed 7-10-15. 2) B. gel mule 3) Black horse with left hind knee had reverted 7-10-15. Black have knee suppurating hero had reverted 7-10-15.	

Place	Date	Hour	Summary of Events and Information	Remarks and references to Appendices
WINCHELSEA	Oct 5		77 Co R.E.	
			(4) Brown mare with fractured Rib off side Chest evacuated 7-10-15.	
			7 EAST YORKS.	
			(5) Brown geelding off hind evacuated 7-10-15.	
			10. WEST YORKS.	
			(6) Br. horse mare Sick her for evacuated 7-10-15.	
			(7) Br. gelt. horse. Sick her for evacuated 7-10-15.	
			(8) Bay gelt horse Injury near shoulder evacuated 7-10-15.	
			146. Co A.S.C.	
			(9) Bright gelt. with laminitis evacuated 7-10-15.	
			6. DORSETS.	
			(10) Chestnut gelt. Kick off thigh evacuated 7-10-15.	
			57. INFANTRY BDE.	
			(11) Br. mare Splint near fore evacuated 7-10-15.	
			78 Bde. Amm. Col.	
			(12) Black gelt. Rope gall off fore evacuated 7-10-15.	

WAR DIARY or INTELLIGENCE SUMMARY

Army Form C. 2118

32.

Instructions regarding War Diaries and Intelligence Summaries are contained in F.S. Regs., Part II. and the Staff Manual respectively. Title Pages will be prepared in manuscript.

(Erase heading not required.)

Place	Date	Hour	Summary of Events and Information	Remarks and references to Appendices
RENINGHELST	Oct. 5	—	Anti-Aircraft Sect. (13) Bty. ged. Artillerie new hind fellows renovated 7-10-15. (14) Br. ged. Steam ligament. head fore-renovated 7-10-15. 148. Co. A.S.C. (15) Br. ged. Detailers renovated 7-10-15. (16) Br. ged. Cachectual that destroyed also Rutter renovated 7-10-15. DISCHARGED:- (1). C. Btty. 81. Bde. Horse Injury to Eyelid (2). D)/90 Bde. R.F.A 5 Horses admitted to Section 1. Horse Discharged.	
RENINGHELST AND GODEWAERSVELDE	6.	4 P.M.	at 4.P.m. Section moved from point 52.C.d.31 (Map 28) with the transport for rest to R.I.C. at railway level crossing (Map 27) arriving at 7.P.M GODEWAERSVELDE. Handed over to in coming Section at farm at RENINGHELST 4 Gunters 4 hand re fu stabling 91 Saucer Sheets and some class of horse Sheets Horse ammunition :- 1. C. Bty. 80. Bde. R.F.A Bandage burst with a furuncan head and some Shudder renovated 7-10-15.	

Army Form C. 2118

WAR DIARY
or
INTELLIGENCE SUMMARY
(Erase heading not required.)

33

Place	Date	Hour	Summary of Events and Information	Remarks and references to Appendices
GODEWAERSVELDE.	Oct. 6		Continued	
			2. Military Police. 17 Div. Brown gun horse contused near knee. Evacuated 7.10.15	
			3. B Bty. 80 Bde. R.F.A. Black horse with wound punctured thigh (off) Evacuated 7-10-15.	
			4. B Bty. 80 Bde. R.F.A. Bay horse hot contused nr fore knee. Evacuated 7-10-15.	
			5. 148 Co. A.S.C. Bay horse with a strand nr his fore foot. Evacuated 7-10-15. Rhotopa. Round suffering from Lupinus Haemorrhagica.	
	7.		O.C. 2 N.C.O's and 10 men proceeded to GODEWAERSVELDE Station to entrain 20 horses and 7 mules to No. 10 VETERINARY HOSPITAL NEUFCHATEL. 1 N.C.O and 4 men no something hurry. 5 horses admitted into section. 2 horses discharged as cured from section.	
			1) Vet. Sect. 17. Div. Amm. Col. Bay gld. with Kust horse contused off hind Evacuated 7-10-15.	
			2. 17. Signal Co. Bay gld. with raper hutr. Evacuated 7-10-15.	

Army Form C. 2118

WAR DIARY
or
INTELLIGENCE SUMMARY

(Erase heading not required.)

Instructions regarding War Diaries and Intelligence Summaries are contained in F.S. Regs., Part II. and the Staff Manual respectively. Title Pages will be prepared in manuscript.

34.

Place	Date	Hour	Summary of Events and Information	Remarks and references to Appendices
DEW RESVE	Oct. 7		Continued.	
			3) C. Bty. 81 Bde. R.F.A.	
			Bay. two wounds Evacuated O.P. One Evacuated 7-10-15.	
			4) 12. Manchester. Regt.	
			Bay. two - Debility - Evacuated 7-10-15.	
			5) A.D.V.S. 17 Div.	
			Shot. two - Exhaustion. Discharged Cured 11-10-15.	
			Discharged Cured.	
			1. 146. Co. A.S.C.	
			2. C/91 Bde. R.F.A.	
"	8		Section Routine	
"	9		Six horses and one mule admitted to Section.	
			1) 7 Lincolns. Regt.	
			Brown horse with Strangles Discharged Cured 19-10-15.	
			2) 10. Lancs. Fusiliers.	
			Bay. horse - Sprain Shoulder Muscles Evacuated 11-10-15.	
			3) 9. Northumberland. Fusiliers.	
			Brown horse with debility Evacuated 11-10-15.	
			4) Amm. Col. 80. Bde. R.F.A.	
			Blue Roan with Debility. Evacuated 11-10-15.	

1875 Wt. W593/826 1,000,000 4/15 J.B.C. & A. A.D.S.S./Forms/C. 2118.

WAR DIARY or INTELLIGENCE SUMMARY

Army Form C. 2118

35.

Place	Date	Hour	Summary of Events and Information	Remarks and references to Appendices
DE WAERSVELDE	Oct. 9.		1) Amm. Col. 80 Bde. R.F.A. Brown geld - Debility - Evacuated 11-10-15. D. Bty. 80 Bde. R.F.A. (a) Black mare with King bart - Evacuated 11-10-15 (b) Bay geld. Buston. Evacuated 11-10-15	
"	10		12 Horses and 1 mule admitted to Section. C. Bty. 81 Bde. R.F.A. Brown mare - Debility - Evacuated 11-10-15. (1) Bay geld - Debility — do (2) Bay mare - Debility — do (3) Bay geld - Debility — do (4) Bay geld - Debility — do 146. Co. A.S.C. (6) Bay mare - Ricked left hind. N. Fore. Evacuated 11-10-15 D. Bty. 81 Bde. R.F.A. (7) Black geld - Debility - Evacuated 11-10-15 (8) Bay geld - Debility — do (9) Bay mare - Debility — do (10) Brown geld - Debility — do	

Army Form C. 2118

36.

WAR DIARY
or
INTELLIGENCE SUMMARY

(Erase heading not required.)

Instructions regarding War Diaries and Intelligence
Summaries are contained in F. S. Regs., Part II.
and the Staff Manual respectively. Title Pages
will be prepared in manuscript.

Place	Date	Hour	Summary of Events and Information	Remarks and references to Appendices
GODEWAERSVELDE	Oct 10		CONTINUED	
			7th East Yorks.	
			1) Brown geld. mule with Strain. Evacuated 11-10-15	
			2) Bay mare with Ind.mus hitherto. do do	
			3) Bay geld with debility. Destroyed. And 10 under treatment no animal has not considered so fit for Evacuation	
	11	12.45 pm	O.C. 2 N.C.O.'s and other proceeded to GODEWAERSVELDE Station to entrain 18 horses and 2 mules for No.10. VETERINARY HOSPITAL.	
			I.N.C.O. and 4 men as con du ching party.	
			8 horses admitted to Section Sick Lines. 1 discharged as cured. admissions:-	
			1) 24. Divisional Artillery.	
			Bay mare with Rope Gall and Evacuated 11-10-15.	
			2) 17 Signal Co.	
			Dun mare with Ins Bones & Evacuated 11-10-15.	
			3) Hq. 80 Bde. R.F.A.	
			Bay mare with Injury Evacuated 14-10-15.	
			4) Bty 81 Bde. R.F.A.	
			4) Bay geld with Debility & Evacuated 14-10-15.	
			5. Bay geld do do And 10 under treatment	
			6 Brown geld do do Evacuated 14-10-15	
			7 dun geld do do no under treatment.	
			8 Bay mare do do Evacuated 14-10-15	

WAR DIARY or INTELLIGENCE SUMMARY

Army Form C. 2118

37

Place	Date	Hour	Summary of Events and Information	Remarks and references to Appendices
GODEWAERSVELDE	Oct 11.		Discharged. A.D.V.S. - Black gd. admitted with Exhaustion 7-10-15	
GODEWAERSVELDE STEENWOORDE	Oct 11.	3-30 P.M.	Section moved complete from GODEWAERSVELDE to near STEENWOORDE. Refer to map Sheet 27. Square Q.8.c.2.8. arriving at 4-45 P.M. O.C and I have moved to farm of Mr CONDEDVILLE-LAMM on HERZEELE on HERZEELE-WORMHOUDT Road to collect horse left by No 36 mobile. Veterinary. Section. Belgian Inspector - marched no longer. G. Five arrived to do duty with the Section. 4 Horses admitted to Section. Amm. Col. 81. Bde. 1) Bay gd. hit below knee; no form of lameness - had and was returned for treatment Yorkshire Dragoons 2) Chestnut gd. with slight following lameness - was returned M O.S 53 Field Ambulance. 3) Black gd. with Ringworm returned for treatment 36. Mob. Vet. Sect. 4) Horse cull C/a Bay gd. who had had pneumonia and was returned as not standing over for 36 Mobile Veterinary Section.	
STEENWOORDE	Oct 12.			

Army Form C. 2118
38.

WAR DIARY
or
INTELLIGENCE SUMMARY
(Erase heading not required.)

Instructions regarding War Diaries and Intelligence Summaries are contained in F.S. Regs., Part II. and the Staff Manual respectively. Title Pages will be prepared in manuscript.

Place	Date	Hour	Summary of Events and Information	Remarks and references to Appendices
TRAIN WOOD RDE.	Oct. 13.		1 horse admitted to Section. 77. Co. R.E. Brown mule with Strain.	
"	14	11am	O.C. 2 N.C.O's and Groom proceeded to CAESTRE Station to entrain 5 horses and 1 mule to No 10 VETERINARY HOSPITAL one N.C.O and horse as Coach and Party.	
			8 horses admitted to Section. Two casting from Section. Admissions:-	
			No 1. Sect. 17 DAC	
			1) Staff horse Influenza Bronco. Evacuated 17-10-15.	
			2) 5th Infantry Bde. Brown mare mule - Kick - horse had a marked lam. Evacuated 17-10-15.	
			A. Btty. 79 Bde. R.F.A	
			3) Chestnut geld horse new hire - Evacuated 17-10-15	
			Amm Col. 81. Bde. R.F.A	
			4) Black mare - Congestion of the Brain - Destroyed.	
			No change.	
			Horse to 36 hvt. Vet. Section	
"	15	-	5 horses admitted to Section.	
			3 Sect. 17 Div. Amm. Col.	
			D. Grey geld mule cast by Remounts & open for Vice - Evacuated 17-10-15	
			do do do do do	

Army Form C. 2118

WAR DIARY
or
INTELLIGENCE SUMMARY
(Erase heading not required.)

39.

Instructions regarding War Diaries and Intelligence Summaries are contained in F. S. Regs., Part II. and the Staff Manual respectively. Title Pages will be prepared in manuscript.

Place	Date	Hour	Summary of Events and Information	Remarks and references to Appendices
STEENWOORDE	Oct. 15.		continued.	
			1) O² Sherwood Foresters:-	
			2) Brown gred. Cast for Vice by Remount Officer. Evacuated 17-10-15.	
			C.Bhy. 79 Bde. R.F.A	
			4) Bay gield with wound up nail. Evacuated 17-10-15.	
			One horse and one mule admired to section.	
			Amm Col. 78 Bde R.F.A.	
			1) Chesnut geld with Sore Bones. Evacuated 20-10-15.	
			2) Brown geld - mule with injury to fort two him. Evacuated 20-10-15	
	16		O.C. 2 N.Co's. and 6 men to CAESTRE Station to entrain 5 horses and 2 mules to No.10. VETERINARY. HOSPITAL. IN.C.O. and 1 men as too on the etron 9 party.	
			5 Horses admired into section.	
			C.Bty. 80. Bde. R.F.A.	
	17		1) Bay geld. Laminitis evacuated 20-10-15.	
			2) Bay horse - Debility do do	
			3) Bay geld - Debility do do	
			4) Bay horse - Debility do do	
			5) Chestnut geld Debility do do	

1875 Wt. W593/826 1,000,000 4/15 J.B.C. & A. A.D.S.S./Forms/C. 2118.

Army Form C. 2118

WAR DIARY
or
INTELLIGENCE SUMMARY

(Erase heading not required.)

Instructions regarding War Diaries and Intelligence Summaries are contained in F.S. Regs., Part II and the Staff Manual respectively. Title Pages will be prepared in manuscript.

Place	Date	Hour	Summary of Events and Information	Remarks and references to Appendices
STEENWOORDE	Oct. 18.		22 horses admitted to Section.	
"	19.		Buttress all those in No 1 alleviated. Injuring horses from No. Gun. 23 horses admitted to Section. Horses – Animals knackery deliverata. As usual of infection by axis. 1 horse destroyed – fed arona filt stock nit open joint. 1 horse discharged cured.	
"	20	11am.	O.C. 2 N.C.O's and 16 men proceeded to CAESTRE Station to entrain for No. 10. Veterinary Hospital. 48 horses and 1 mule. 1 N.C.O and 7 men as conducting party. 1 horse destroyed and 4 horses admitted to Section. 1 horse discharged cured.	
"	21		4 horses and 1 mule admitted to Section. 2 horses destroyed. One had case of Tetanus and another Fact. Open Knee Joint.	

WAR DIARY
or
INTELLIGENCE SUMMARY

Army Form C. 2118

Place	Date	Hour	Summary of Events and Information	Remarks and references to Appendices
STEENWOORDE	Oct 22		4 Horses admitted to Le chien.	
"	23		O.C. 2 N.C.O's and 5 men proceeded to CAESTRE Station to entrain Horses and 1 mule to NO. 10 VETERINARY HOSPITAL 1 N.C.O and 1 man as conducting party. 2 Horses admitted to Section. 1 N.C.O and 2 men proceeded to REMOUNT DEPOT (ADVANCED) to bring back for Nneron 5 Remounts.	
STEENWOORDE	24	12.30 pm	Section ordered to proceed from O.E.C. 2.8 Sheet 27 Rest billet to Nneronal area. Section moved complete straight along to Nneronal area. Section moved sick animals and animals under going treatment. Route was along Poperin Road – STEENWOORDE ABEELE – POPERINGHE.	
POPERINGHE	"	3.15 pm	Section arrived at new area. hut Sheet 27. L. 29 b 7. 9 the huts no erected but the roads good: while section and 3 horses here I horse was left with N.8.C. Mobile Le chien taken over from No.M. Mobile. Le chien Erected cover for all the section horses from advanced bivouacs. Owing to the rainy weather can't hue in a very	
"	"			

WAR DIARY or INTELLIGENCE SUMMARY

Army Form C. 2118

Place	Date	Hour	Summary of Events and Information	Remarks and references to Appendices
OPERINGHE	Oct. 25		Muddy state and footways had to be made. Owing to want of refugees accommodation was limited.	
"	26		Two big convoys of horses standing awaiting a wind. Been also confused for 45 men. A draft of 16 men arrived to join section from No. 8 Veterinary Hospital. Mule arrived to section.	
"	27		When left the section and proceeded to No. 8 P. Veterinary Hospital. Sent out of fatigues party to clean & heal away / condition. Junk for 45 men was bad. Horse admitted to section.	
"	28		9 horses admitted to section. 1 discharge cured. 3 horses admitted to section.	
"	29			
"	30		Three choclen Fd. Cured, Weak still very bad and condition of camp also. Ligure but nobre out stormed roads. Returning from in a bad state.	

N.C.O. (Sgt. REEVE) Proceeded on 7days leave of absence to England.

Army Form C. 2118

43.

WAR DIARY
or
INTELLIGENCE SUMMARY
(Erase heading not required.)

Instructions regarding War Diaries and Intelligence Summaries are contained in F. S. Regs., Part II. and the Staff Manual respectively. Title Pages will be prepared in manuscript.

Place	Date	Hour	Summary of Events and Information	Remarks and references to Appendices
POPERINGHE	Oct 31		1 horse admitted to Section, treated conditions seem bad and condition of Camp wet mud very bad also. Ammn we have, if spare hut no sleeping place and hut for men where heats on. Sent to Convalesc. 161. Sent to hired. 10 Sent no. discharges. 7 Total. no. In an Treatments Remaining, 5.	

J.R. Keppel Lieut AV?
OC 29 Mobile Veterinary Section
Nov 1. 1915.

29th Inf. Res. Div.
vol. 5

D/
7678

17th Division

Nov 15.

WAR DIARY or INTELLIGENCE SUMMARY

Army Form C. 2118

29. MOBILE VETERINARY SECTION.

44.

Place	Date	Hour	Summary of Events and Information	Remarks and references to Appendices
POPERINGHE	NOV. 1st		1 horse admitted to Section.	
"	2		I have proceeded on leave of absence to England. Corporal Erection of Staff in stables and places for him.	
"	3		1 horse admitted to Section. Received telephonic message to have one of Section billets (at L.29.b.7.9.) by 12.00 noon the 3rd of November. The position taken over from the outgoing unit was found to be on the 9th Divisional area and they intimated we had to leave. Sent messengers to inform those concerned through the Divisional troops and batteries had to be abandoned as well as the Station and horses for the coming winter.	
"	"	12-30 pm	Section moved complete to new site on the POPERINGHE-RENINGHELST Road in Map Sheet 28.C.14.b.2.5. Great difficulty to obtain a suitable site owing to the fact that almost all the ground was already occupied.	
"	4		1 horse admitted to Section	
"	5		O.C. 2 N.C.O.S. and 5 men proceed to POPERINGHE Station & received 3 horses and 2 mules from No.10. VETERINARY HOSPITAL NEUFCHATEL. 1 N.C.O. and 1 man to conducting parties.	

Army Form C. 2118

Mobile Veterinary Section
45.

WAR DIARY
or
INTELLIGENCE SUMMARY
(Erase heading not required.)

Place	Date	Hour	Summary of Events and Information	Remarks and references to Appendices
POPERINGHE.	Nov 6		1 horse and 1 mule admitted Section. 1 horse discharged cured. Received orders to Mallow Post-mortem on horse suspected of GLANDERS 5 horses of C. Bty. 79. Bde. R.F.A. hide bot-mortem on horse suspected of GLANDERS. No internal lesions in Tarcy. Buds. Ulceration of Schneiderian mucous membrane.	
"	7		Inspected trained horses of C/79. R.F.A. and performed Leto Mareal palpation test on horses. No reactions to this date. 1 man sent to England	
"	8		Inspected 42 horses with mules at C/79. R.F.A. 1 horse hand to England. 4 horses gave a good reaction to the Leto Mareal Palpation method. These animals had been injected on the 6th inst. by the Intra-dermal method. Had given no reaction. Post mortem revealed very advanced cases of GLANDERS lesions from haemorrhagic spots to tubercle twigs of a pea size participating in all 4 cases.	
"	9		Inspected with mules 29 horses of C/79. R.F.A.	
"	10		O.C. 2 N.co's and 4 men proceeded to POPERINGHE Station to entrain for NO.10. VETERINARY. HOSPITAL. NEUFCHATEL 1 horse and 2 Mules 1 N.C.O and 1 man as conducting party.	
"	11		1 horse admitted Section	

Army Form C. 2118

WAR DIARY
or
INTELLIGENCE SUMMARY
(Erase heading not required.)

Instructions regarding War Diaries and Intelligence Summaries are contained in F. S. Regs., Part II and the Staff Manual respectively. Title Pages will be prepared in manuscript.

Place	Date	Hour	Summary of Events and Information	Remarks and references to Appendices
POPERINGHE	Nov 12		2 Horses admitted to Section	
"	13		1 Horse admitted to Section	
"	14		—	
"	15		6 horses admitted to Section	
"	16		O.C. proceeded with 2 N.C.O.s and 5 men to POPERINGHE Station to entrain 9 horses & mules to N.O.10 Veterinary Hospital. 1 N.C.O. and 2 men as conducting party.	
"			1 Horse destroyed	
"			6 horses admitted to Section	
"	17	9.30 pm	3 horses admitted to Section. Called out suddenly to Inkerman on horse at No.116 Co. R.E. Proceeded to 116 Co. camp with Sgt. REEVE and found big Shire horse kicking with its greatest difficulty from passing on train from a deep central sharp quiver abscess. opened. Indian mounts mule.	
"	18		2 horses and 4 horses admitted to Section	
"	19		O.C. 2 N.C.O.s and 1 men proceed to POPERINGHE Station to entrain for No.10. VETERINARY HOSPITAL 9 horses and 2 mules. 1 N.C.O. and 1 man as conducting party. 3 horses admitted to Section	

Army Form C. 2118

29 Mobile Section
47

WAR DIARY
or
INTELLIGENCE SUMMARY
(Erase heading not required.)

Instructions regarding War Diaries and Intelligence Summaries are contained in F. S. Regs., Part II. and the Staff Manual respectively. Title Pages will be prepared in manuscript.

Place	Date	Hour	Summary of Events and Information	Remarks and references to Appendices
POPERINGHE	Nov 19		1. Sergeant - promoted Staff Sergeant.	
			1. Corporal - do - Sergeant.	
			1. Shoeing Smith - do - Farrier Sergeant.	
"	20		9 Horses. 1 Mule admitted to Section.	
"	21		9 Horses. 3 Mules admitted to Section	
"	22		O.C. 2 N.C.O's and 12 men proceed to POPERINGHE Station to entrain for NO.10. VETERINARY HOSPITAL 30 horses and 3 mules. 1 N.C.O and 3 men as conducting party.	
			7 horses admitted to Section	
"	23		9 Horses, 3 mules admitted to Section	
			1 Horse died from Pneumonia.	
			A Shoeing Smith joined Section for duty from NO.2 VETERINARY HOSPITAL to replace Shoeing Smith promoted Farrier Sergeant.	
"	24		5 Horses admitted to Section.	
			Farrier Sergeant Brown left for NO. 9 VETERINARY HOSPITAL.	
"	25			

Army Form C. 2118

29 Mobile Section

48.

WAR DIARY
or
INTELLIGENCE SUMMARY
(Erase heading not required.)

Instructions regarding War Diaries and Intelligence Summaries are contained in F.S. Regs., Part II and the Staff Manual respectively. Title Pages will be prepared in manuscript.

Place	Date	Hour	Summary of Events and Information	Remarks and references to Appendices
POPERINGHE	Nov. 26		O.C. 2 N.C.O's and 11 men proceeded to POPERINGHE Station to entrain 18 horses and 2 mules to No. 10 VETERINARY HOSPITAL. 1 N.C.O. 3 men as train conducting party. Two wounded stragglers kept.	
"	27		Came 5 sick h'gs from three spare Poropolis Aerr. Horses admitted to Section.	
"	28		4 horses admitted Section. Horses serving for horses from a Poropolis Aerr.	
"	29		O.C. 2 N.C.O's and 2 men proceeded to POPERINGHE Station to entrain 14 horses and 1 mule to No. 10 VETERINARY HOSPITAL. 1 N.C.O. and 3 men as train conducting party. Horses admitted to Section.	
"	30		3 horses admitted to Section. 1 sick dung night from horse.	

30-11-15.
G Russell Orr
O.C. 29 Mobile Veterinary Section

29. Hub. Feb. detr.
Vol. 8

D/
7835.

Army Form C. 2118

WAR DIARY
or
INTELLIGENCE SUMMARY
(Erase heading not required.)

29 Mobile Veterinary Section
17 Division
December 1915

Place	Date	Hour	Summary of Events and Information	Remarks and references to Appendices
POPERINGHE	Dec. 1st		3 horses admitted to Section. Inspected 29 horses at C/79 R.F.A. with trainer – L-Cpl Vernal Palpebral Test	
"	2		2 horses admitted to Section. O.C. 2 NCO's and 4 men proceeded to POPERINGHE Station to entrain 10 horses and 1 mule for No.10 VETERINARY HOSPITAL. 1 NCO and 1 man as train conducting party	
"	3		4 horses admitted to Section. Inspected 26 horses at C/79 R.F.A. with trainer – L-Cpl Lapshane Test	
"	4		3 horses admitted to Section. Inspected 39 horses with trainer at C/79 R.F.A. 1 Reactor from bat C 3-12-15 destroyed and post-mortem made. Lesion of Glands found in Lungs – tubercle. Tuang's sign. 3 horses admitted to Section. Inspected C/79 R.F.A. 35 horses with trainer – Eye Test	
"	5			
"	6		4 horses H mules admitted to Section lines. O.C. 3 N.C.O's and 4 men proceeded to POPERINGHE Station to entrain	

J B Stinson L.V.
O.C. 29 M.V.S.

WAR DIARY or INTELLIGENCE SUMMARY

Page 2.

Place	Date	Hour	Summary of Events and Information	Remarks and references to Appendices
POPERINGHE N.O.	6		9 horses and 1 mule for NO.10 VETERINARY HOSPITAL. 1 N.C.O. and 2 men as conducting party. Proceeded to H.Q. 14 Div to assist A.D.V.S. of that formation to perform the Intra-Palpebral test for Glanders. Infected 57 horses & mules.	
"	7		8 horses and 1 mule admitted to section. 1 horse also cast as incurable. Destroyed. Proceeded to 47th Siege R.G.A. accompanied by N.C.O. as ordered and tested the horses there with Intra-Palpebral test for A.D.V.S. 14 Div.	
"	8		O.C. 2 N.C.O's. 11 men proceeded to POPERINGHE Station to entrain 17 horses and 6 mules for NO.13 VETERINARY HOSPITAL. 1 N.C.O. and 3 men train party. 11 horses and 1 mule admitted to section. 2 horses also cast as incurable.	
"	9		2 Horses admitted to section here. The weather from the 3rd to the 9th intensely wet, standard conditions of constant very hard work. The large numbers of animals which makes the work of the men hard arduous.	

WAR DIARY
or
INTELLIGENCE SUMMARY

(Erase heading not required.)

Army Form C. 2118

3.

Place	Date	Hour	Summary of Events and Information	Remarks and references to Appendices
POPERINGHE	Dec 10.		2 horses admitted to Section	
"	11		Sgt Griffin S.E.Bush examined a bad foot from his horse though Cocoa on nt a hole can owing to the little skin on the feet have been rendered effective	
"	12		O.C. 2 N.C.O's and 6 men proceeded to POPERINGHE Station to entrain 10 horses + mules to No.13 VETERINARY Hospital. 1 N.C.O 2 men as train party. Weather very wet 13 horses admitted to Section	
"	12		nil	
"	13		O.C. 2 N.C.O's and Men proceeded to POPERINGHE Station to entrain 16 horses to No.13 VETERINARY HOSPITAL. 1 N.C.O and 4 men as train party	
"	14		3 horses and 2 mules admitted to Section 1 horse discharged Cured. A.D.V.S. proceed on leave and took over his duties as well as Section	

WAR DIARY or INTELLIGENCE SUMMARY

Army Form C. 2118

Place	Date	Hour	Summary of Events and Information	Remarks and references to Appendices
POPERINGHE	Dec. 15		3 horses/mules admitted to section. Devoted afternoon to movement H.Q. at RENINGHELST and attended to office duties of A.D.V.S.	
"	16		O.C 2 N.CO's and 1 man to POPERINGHE Station between them & No. 13 VETERINARY HOSPITAL. 1 N.CO. and 2 men to transport party. Proceeded to H.Q. 6th Division (17) and attended to office duties. Interview D.M.S. about presence of manure in horse lines of Division and discussed preventive measures.	
"	17		10 horses/mules admitted to section. Attended at 17 Div. Amm. Col. with D.D.V.S. IInd Army to meet horses for reserve & other than Veterinary at H.Q. Division afternoon and interviewed G.O.C. about horses of their command as to their condition and fitness for any breath and pointed out that they might be put to.	
"	18		O.C 3 N.CO's and 10 men proceeded to POPERINGHE Station to entrain 23 horses and 1 mule to No. 13 VETERINARY HOSPITAL (N.CO. & men to train party).	

Army Form C. 2118

WAR DIARY
or
INTELLIGENCE SUMMARY
(Erase heading not required.)

Place	Date	Hour	Summary of Events and Information	Remarks and references to Appendices
POPERINGHE	Dec. 18.		Proceeded from to A.D. Division of A.D.V.S. and Routine Muster. 7 Horses. 3 hules admitted to section.	
"	19	4.30 am	2 Horses admitted to Section. Proceeded from O. to A.D. Division to have act office duties. Section ordered to stand to Arms at 4-30 A.M. by O.C. owing to the Bombardment of POPERINGHE by the enemy. The early morning shelling fell short of the town and landed around the Section encampment, some of the shells being in the next field a distance of a few yards away. The loud sound of the Explosions the flying debris caused great uneasiness amongst the horses escape which for the time being were guiding enough. The Bombardment lasted all the day there being right at intervals but no more shells came near the section. He was the primary exposure shell or Thunder of a 6 inch shell. At 9am enemy aeroplanes made their appearance and there were seen to be followed by our & two enemy	

WAR DIARY or INTELLIGENCE SUMMARY

Army Form C. 2118

Place	Date	Hour	Summary of Events and Information	Remarks and references to Appendices
POPERINGHE	DEC 19.		Aeroplanes were seen engaged with two of our machines and during low from them headed right over the Station and dropped a big bomb each - fortunately a huy miss was behind the Station. Flash went the bombs hit the ground & the pieces went somers sailing to the air no damage was done.	
"	20		Three enemy aeroplanes advised to section. Located afternoon to H.Q. Division for Duties as A.D.S. During the night the enemy again bombarded the town and having got up close to the Station (where I was camped also) I observed the shell after I was sure that the enemy shell were hitting the town and in falling short as before. Located the Division for Antwp. Staff U.S. Intercom Amb. alone, watching Y.Pres and the four evacuations from here.	
"	21		Three advised to section. Morning at H.Q. Antwp for Antwp F.A.D.S. The enemy again shelled POPERINGHE during the night. The enemy again shelled POPERINGHE during the night but sent no cases for Antwp as the Shells? was Slight soon stopped but sent to cause for alarm and very well carried out all orders	

WAR DIARY or INTELLIGENCE SUMMARY

Army Form C. 2118

Place	Date	Hour	Summary of Events and Information	Remarks and references to Appendices
POPERINGHE	Dec 21		Acted if Adjutant in a complicated manner til was very gratifying to see & to know that the men could do exercises as to some it had been just that there been & should have made.	
"	22		O.C. 2 N.C.O.S. 11 men to POPERINGHE Station to entrain 95 horses and 5 mules to No.13 VETERINARY HOSPITAL. 1 NCO 4 men as train party.	
"	23		Proceeded afternoon to H.Q. Division, divers fairs.	
"	9/11		1 horse 3 mules admitted to Section. 3 mules admitted at Vet. Hosp/Section. H.Q. Division horses & - duties ADVS. 4 mules admitted sector. 1 mule discharged as Cured.	
"	25		Proceeded H.Q. Division & afternoon this aft. over to A.D.V.S. On his return from leave. 1 horse discharged Cured	
"	26		3 horses admitted section	

WAR DIARY or INTELLIGENCE SUMMARY

Army Form C. 2118

Place	Date	Hour	Summary of Events and Information	Remarks and references to Appendices
POPERINGHE	Nov 27.		1 horse admitted to Section.	
"	28.		16 Horses admitted to Section	
"	29.		O.C. 3 N.C.O's and 10 men proceeded to POPERINGHE Station to entrain 20 animals for No. 13 VETERINARY Hospital. NEUFCHATEL. 1 N.C.O and 3 men as conducting party. 15 Horses admitted to the Section. Enemy Bombed town of POPERINGHE in afternoon.	
"	30.		17 Animals admitted to Section. Enemy put some shells into POPERINGHE. A few fell short and some did not burst.	
"	31.		32 Animals admitted to the Section. The front line very trying on the men of the Section owing to the bad weather conditions. The muddy condition with the rain caused the horses to be in a bad state and this with the large number of animals for Evacuation and newly all cases surgical required more aid than the short day admits and in every act of dressing and Pin to the Section had applied which entailed some of the men worked at our disposal have worked continuously and willingly and have most cheerfully and under exceptionally trying conditions at POPERINGHE Station here. The shewing of own animals that were found healthy and when a number of trucks were found not good and when a number of animals to be thought fit to travel siding for needed coverings from front to front siding to entring	

WAR DIARY
or
INTELLIGENCE SUMMARY

Army Form C. 2118

Place	Date	Hour	Summary of Events and Information	Remarks and references to Appendices
POPERINGHE	Dec. 31		24 hours notice must be given for trucks where there is hours breed be sufficient as I found out that where I gave the R.T.O. 24 hours notice the R.O.D. sent out 12 hours from the R.T.O. intimating the number of horses for a railway truck viz:- 6 Heavy draught and 8 light draught to a truck. The Veterinary Officer ought to be the last to say if first class animals belong to and not as the R.T.O. informed me that he was the "best judge" and some heavy draught horses I had for trucking he declared as being "medium." There is need for improvement in the railing of horses from this station.	

J Stennel Lieut RVC
O.C. 29 Mobile Vet[?] Section
Dec 31. 1915.

29th Mobile Vet Section
17th Division
Vol: VII

Adjutant General's
Office
The Base.

Attached War Diary
for January — Owing
to my absence in
Hospital with
injury to hand I
could not write
up diary sooner.

J.J. Stenhel
Capt.
O C 29 M V S

O.C.
29 MOBILE VETERINARY
SECTION.

Army Form C. 2118

WAR DIARY
or
INTELLIGENCE SUMMARY

(Erase heading not required.)

Instructions regarding War Diaries and Intelligence Summaries are contained in F. S. Regs, Part II and the Staff Manual respectively. Title Pages will be prepared in manuscript.

Place	Date	Hour	Summary of Events and Information	Remarks and references to Appendices
POPERINGHE	Jan 1	10 am	O.C., 3 N.C.O's and 15 men proceeded to POPERINGHE Station to entrain 43 horses and 8 mules for No. 13 VETERINARY HOSPITAL NEUFCHATEL. 1 N.C.O and 6 men as conducting party. 8 horses admitted to Section.	
"	Jan 2		9 horses and 2 mules admitted to Section	
"	3		14 horses admitted to Section	
"	4		9 horses admitted to Section	
"	5	10 am	O.C. 3 N.C.O's and 15 men proceeded to POPERINGHE Station to entrain 51 horses to No. 13. VETERINARY HOSPITAL. 1 N.C.O and 6 men as conducting party. 2 horses admitted to Section	
"	6		Section standing by to preparing to moving out to the	
"	7		rest area.	
"	8	2 pm	Section proceeded on line of march to TILQUES near ST OMER. Section started at 2 PM. At STEENWOORDE the first halting place was reached, had spent a good farm house with sufficient accommodation for men and horses. Rested at this farm as a billet.	

WAR DIARY or INTELLIGENCE SUMMARY

Army Form C. 2118

Place	Date	Hour	Summary of Events and Information	Remarks and references to Appendices
POPERINGHE to STEENWOORDE	Jun 9		The first portion of this march was done in good time owing to the good state of repair of the road with minimum amount of traffic. No casualties to men or horses.	
STEENWOORDE to TILQUES.	Jun 9	7.30 am	Section proceeded on its line of march via CASSEL to BAVINCHOVE to ZUYTPEENE where a halt was called to water and feed horses also men's dinner. 2 horses was allowed when animals were saddled up and draught yokes in when section proceeded via L'HEY to COIN PERDU to CLAIR MARAIS through ST OMER along the CANAL bank to main road for CALAIS and halted at TILQUES our destination arriving 5 pm.	
		5 pm	The Section had a very good march for such a long journey. Horses then travelling well the animals pulled up at the finish showing little fatigue - not a shoe was cast no men fell out. The day was a real test for the roads were in a good state of repair. The hill over CASSEL HILL had a severe one for the haflon horses but it proved their loads well it proved to watered.	

P. Rushworth
Lt 4/MS

WAR DIARY or INTELLIGENCE SUMMARY

Army Form C. 2118

Place	Date	Hour	Summary of Events and Information	Remarks and references to Appendices
TILQUES.	Jan 9		The Billets in the huts at TILQUES were excellent for men and horses. The Bivouacs were occupied & the large sheds to the Bivouac afforded excellent stabling for the horses and it was good to see the horses done over then week and conditions as when at POPERINGHE the conditions if put to the Camp was awful a little work came to clear the Section horses in consequence and also things (numbers) of animals that came for evacuation kept the section twenty working. S.	
"	Jan 10.		9 animals admitted to Section	
"	11		4 horses admitted to Section	
"	12		8 horses admitted to Section. O.C. 2 N.C.O's and 7 men proceeded to WATTEN Station to entrain horses for No. 13 VETERINARY HOSPITAL. IN. C.O. and 2 horses for conducting party.	
"	13.	6 a.m.	The O.C. proceeded on leave of absence to England (Lieut J.E. KEPPEL arr.) The A.V.S. W.503/826 N.1670² W.NEALE H.U.C. carrying on in charge of Section.	

Army Form C. 2118

Instructions regarding War Diaries and Intelligence Summaries are contained in F. S. Regs., Part II and the Staff Manual respectively. Title Pages will be prepared in manuscript.

WAR DIARY
or
INTELLIGENCE SUMMARY

(Erase heading not required.)

Place	Date	Hour	Summary of Events and Information	Remarks and references to Appendices
TILQUES.	Jan 13-21		On leave.	
"	22.		11 Horses 1 mule admitted to Section	
"	23		6 horses 4 mules admitted to Section	
"	24		4 horses admitted to Section	
			O.C. 1 N.C.O. and 4 men collected horses at BROZEELE left by the 9th Division on a line of March.	
"	25		O.C. 2 N.C.O's and 12 men proceeded to WATTEN Station to entrain 23 horses admitted for NO.13 VETERINARY HOSPITAL.	
			1 N.C.O and 5 men as conducting party	
			4 horses and 1 mule admitted to Section	
"	26		9 horses admitted to Section	
"	27		O.C. 1 N.C.O and 4 men collecting horses and carrying out Schedules. Have learnt forms horses collected in our (6th) War Horse reserve are tags from Section H.A. 6 horses collected which were left by 9th D. division.	

1875 W¹ W593/826 1,000,000 4/15 J.B.C. & A. A.D.S.S./Forms/C. 2118.

WAR DIARY or INTELLIGENCE SUMMARY

Army Form C. 2118

Place	Date	Hour	Summary of Events and Information	Remarks and references to Appendices
TILQUES	Sept 27		O.C. (Lieut. J.J.G. KEPPEL) hallowed the horses & mules of the 17. Div. Amm. Column and whilst inserting the needle into an animal made the animal forget & the men holding it. As the animal go with the Hypodermic syringe attached to its eye so to save the animal from injury to eye also the syringe from injury since KEPPEL seized animals head and withdrew syringe but in the act of withdrawance of the syringe the animal reared up. The syringe fell point on & their Kneels here however being stuck on the syringe drove the needle further into its stuff leaving it imbedded. After this 2.O animals were caught without further care possible here but 57 of field Ambulance was the O.C. assisted out & arranged for X.Ray examination at St.OMER.	
TILQUES	Sept 28		O.C. proceeded in Ambulance to ST OMER where his X-Rays & much located. O.C. returned as patient In Hospital	
	Sept 28-31		In Hospital	

J.S. Kendal Capt.Aus.
O.C. 17. M.V.S.

29ten Indr: Vet: Sect:
vol: 8

17

Army Form C. 2118

29. MOBILE VETERINARY SECTION

WAR DIARY or INTELLIGENCE SUMMARY

(Erase heading not required.)

Vol. I

Place	Date	Hour	Summary of Events and Information February 1916.	Remarks and references to Appendices
TILQUES	Feb 1-6.		At Hospital St Omer.	
NOIR-CARME	6.		Left Tilques owing to division moving back to the front as unable to travel with section owing to H.Q. of 14th Army taking Tilques. Then remained at Station for but a few hours notice to evacuate then the Section got but a diet of horses Section moved into a farm Billet. After a diet of horses Section moved into a farm near 2 v. DAUSQUES as NOIR CARME and there awaits orders to move back to front.	
"	7.		6 horses & 1 mule admitted to Section.	
"	8.		—	
"	9.		Evacuated to N.O. 13 VETERINARY HOSPITAL. 29 Animals from ST. OMER. 1 horse admitted to section suffering from ophthalmia 1 horse admitted to section suffering from effects of a kick made below the hock got up in a float - my found to have a compound fracture of the Near hind Tibia - & destroyed.	

Army Form C. 2118

WAR DIARY
or
INTELLIGENCE SUMMARY
(Erase heading not required.)

Instructions regarding War Diaries and Intelligence Summaries are contained in F. S. Regs., Part II. and the Staff Manual respectively. Title Pages will be prepared in manuscript.

Place	Date	Hour	Summary of Events and Information	Remarks and references to Appendices
NOIR-CARME	Feb. 11	9am	Section moved from NOIR-CARME to RENINGHELST in rear of 17. Divisional Ammunition Column via MOULLE to ST. MOMELIN to BUSSYCHEURE where the Section halted for the night. Arrived BUSSYCHEURE 2.P.M.	
BUSSYCHEURE to STEENWOORDE.	12	10am	Spare Section left for STEENWOORDE via ZUYTPEENE to CASSEL and thence to STEENWOORDE arriving at 6 P.M. where the Section billeted for the night. At BAVINCHOVE the Section halted to water & feed.	
STEENWOORDE to RENINGHELST	13	9am	the Section left for RENINGHELST via GODEWAERS- VELDE to BOESCHEPE arriving at RENINGHELST and billeting at G.31.b. Sheet 27. The trek over was well done without any casualties of falling out in men or horses. The weather during the frost days' trek was brilliantly clear very cold. the two extra days being for the roads here in a frost condition until we put men the front with a view to get the roads up to put before reaching WESTOUTRE	

Army Form C. 2118

WAR DIARY
or
INTELLIGENCE SUMMARY
(Erase heading not required.)

Place	Date	Hour	Summary of Events and Information	Remarks and references to Appendices
ENINGHELST	13		Until arrival as fillies were very bad. Section arrived 3 P.M. Horses then finishing up feed.	
"	14		Ambulance float arrived. Use of Section as gift from the Royal Society for Prevention of Cruelty to Animals. 1 N.C.O. and 4 horses proceeded to POPERINGHE Station to Escorts to NO. 13 VETERINARY HOSPITAL. 6 horses and 1 mule.	
"	15		1 N.C.O. as Conducting party. Animals in a difficulty in proceeding along the bad surface of the pavé road. 9 horses 1 mule admitted to Section	
"	16		Nil	
"	17		4 horses admitted to Section	
"	18		7 horses and 1 mule admitted to Section	
"	19		O.C. 2 N.C.O.'s and 7 men proceeded to POPERINGHE Station to evacuate 14 horses and 2 mules to No. 13. VETERINARY HOSPITAL. Ambulance float to convey one bad case of Rheum. to Station. 1 N.C.O. and 2 men as Conductors. Great difficulty was experienced in getting it over the bad front road.	

Army Form C. 2118.

WAR DIARY
or
INTELLIGENCE SUMMARY.
(Erase heading not required.)

Instructions regarding War Diaries and Intelligence Summaries are contained in F.S. Regs., Part II. and the Staff Manual respectively. Title pages will be prepared in manuscript.

4.

Place	Date	Hour	Summary of Events and Information	Remarks and references to Appendices
ENINGHELST	Feb 20		I was ordered to Sector. This was a bad case of Quittor from the Amm. Coll. 78 Bde R.F.A. and the Ambulance float was used. The foot had great difficulty in getting in to the Cart owing to its hugeness. After a week treatment in Sector was unable to walk very well to Station was so for hospital.	
"	21		3 horses admitted to Sector.	
"	22		3 horses admitted to Sector. One horse evacuated by foot.	
"	23		6 horses admitted to Sector. One very bad case of Quitor evacuated by float.	
"	24		O.C. 2 N.C.O's and 9 men proceeded to GODEWAERSVELDE Station to entrain horses for NO.13 VETERINARY HOSPITAL Ambulance float conveying one animal. N.C.O and 2 men conducting party. The road to GODEWAERSVELDE through WESTOUTRE-BOESCHEPE road was no heel coming going for the Ambulance.	

T2134. Wt. W708—776. 500090. 4/15. Sir J. C. & S.

WAR DIARY
or
INTELLIGENCE SUMMARY.

Army Form C. 2118.

Place	Date	Hour	Summary of Events and Information	Remarks and references to Appendices
REININGHELST	24		4 horses admitted to Section. One horse brought in Ambulance	
"	25			
"	26		4 horses admitted to Section. One Ambulance case	
"	27		nil	
"	28		8 horses admitted to Section. O.C. 2 N.C.O's and 6 men proceeded to GODEWAERSVELDE Station to entrain 11 horses and 2 horses for No. 13 VETERINARY HOSPITAL. 1 N.C.O and 1 man as Conducting party. 3 horses admitted to Section.	
"	29		The Ambulance float is not suitable for the roads about the Ypres Salient front. The waggon is very heavy and the axle is very low. The waggon is also provided with iron buffers or rests behind that are always touching on the ground when going over uneven and grass surfaces, and has been made not ill-adapted to the work here supporting these rests. When the buffers have to pass on the buddy side of the road tomorrow the wheels have the axle grates along the surface of the ground	

and useless. Carefully driven the axle moved suffer. You owing to the weight of the waggon its single pair [wheel] wheels it is impossible to get it through the roads whoever to many of the horse [mules] the wheels sunk in [during] the body of the [cart] but it [proving] to want of [leverage] the [float] to [take] to [sink].

In [addition] of the float to the equipment of the Section will greatly help in relieving the [wastage] in [horses] as all the [cases] (so far) brought to the Section in the [first] have been [volunteer] animals who with [severe] foot [lesions] and after [evidence] treatment on the Section these animals were so relieved that they walked quite well to the Station at GODEWAERSVELDE a distance of about 7 miles.

13/6.

J.P.Bushnell Capt att
OC79 Mobile Veterinary Section.

17.

29 M.Vet S.

Vol 9

WAR DIARY
or
INTELLIGENCE SUMMARY

Army Form C. 2118.

of 29 Mobile Veterinary Section

Nov ct. 1916.

Place	Date	Hour	Summary of Events and Information	Remarks and references to Appendices
ZENINGHELST	Nov 1		One animal admitted to section. Run for animals - Shew loaned from No.10 Veterinary Hospital.	
"	Nov 2		O.C. I/N.CO. and Shew proceeded to GODEWAERSVELDE Station to entrain 12 horses & 2 mules to No.10. Veterinary Hospital. I/N.CO. and 2 men as conducting parties. O.C. Inspecting horses that were subjected to the mallein test (Intra-Dermal Method of test) at 17 Divisional Train (A.S.C.) at No 748 Co. one animal this case +this has marked that on one site for further test.	
"	3		7 horses & 2 mules admitted to section.	
"	4		4 horses & 2 mules admitted to section. Ambulance float conveyed horse suffering from laminitis from No. 148. C.A.S.C.	
"	5		O.C. taking animals at 17 Divisional Train A.S.C. with Intra-Dermal Mallein test for Glanders.	

WAR DIARY or INTELLIGENCE SUMMARY

Army Form C. 2118.

2. 29. M.V.S.

Place	Date	Hour	Summary of Events and Information	Remarks and references to Appendices
REMINGHELST			O.C. 2 N.CO's and 10 men proceeded to GODEWAERSVELDE Station 16 horses 12 mules. Ambulance conveying one case entrained for N0. 18. Veterinary Hospital. H. C. O. 2 men as Conducting party. 6 horses admitted to Section of which 2 were discharged. Ambulance conveyed above from 146. Coy. A.S.C. O.C. Inspecting billeted horses of 17 Divisional Train.	
"	April 7.		11 horses admitted to Section of which 2 were discharged Ambulance conveyed case for evacuation to GODEWAERSVELDE where it stayed the night with N.O.1. SECT. 17 DIVISIONAL AMMUN-ITION COLUMN. O.C. Inspecting horses of 17. Divisional Train.	
"	" 8		O.C. 2 N.C.O's and 10 men left 21 horses proceeded to GODEWAERSVELDE to entrain horses to NO.18 Veterinary Hospital. Ambulance conveying	

WAR DIARY
or
INTELLIGENCE SUMMARY.

29. M. V. S. Army Form C. 2118.

Place	Date	Hour	Summary of Events and Information	Remarks and references to Appendices
ENING HEIST	March 8		One case & went to N.O.1. Sect. 17. D.A.C. to bring case of horse night. 1 N.O.O. and 3 men as car during trip. O.C. spectig halted horses of 17. Divisional Train. 7 horses admitted to Section.	
"	"	9	4 horses admitted to Section. Ambulance proceed to D/178 Bde. R.H.A. at DICKEBUSH & Convey arrived here by Shell.	
"	"	10	O.C. & N.C.O.'S taken prisoner to COUDEKAERSVELDE Station to entrain 6 horses for 13. Veterinary Hospital. Ambulance conveying one case. 6 horses admitted to Section. 1 Run for event loaned from N.O.4. Veterinary Hospital.	

WAR DIARY or INTELLIGENCE SUMMARY

Army Form C. 2118.

29.11.15

Place	Date	Hour	Summary of Events and Information	Remarks and references to Appendices
PENINGHELST	Nov. 11		O.C. 2 N.C.O's and 3 men proceeded to OSTWAERSVELDE Station to entrain 13 horses to 13 Veterinary Hospital. 1 N.C.O. and 2 men as Conducting party. Ambulance conveyed one case to Station. 3 horses admitted Section of which 2 were sent to station after train party for Evacuation. The third being retained for re - issue to its Unit.	
"	" 17		The Section proceeded after horse portion of Ambulance to CAESTRE. The day was fine. Horses fit to do heavy left Veninghelst Bryde front were fired. The track was soft, and no trouble in reaching time no casualties of falling out. The Ambulance front arriving to its bigger truck was slow - having a great amount of Section Kit carried it was very small & the Wheeled off the Limber G.S. when Ambulance was moved was greatly felt.	
	" 9.30a			

WAR DIARY or INTELLIGENCE SUMMARY

Army Form C. 2118.

Place	Date	Hour	Summary of Events and Information	Remarks and references to Appendices
CAESTRE	March 13		Setting up bullet which had been shaken a bit of great convenience & it was seen that the advantages to be gained from having the section as a near unit had been manifold.	
"	"	14	6 horses admitted to Section	
"	"	15	4 horses admitted to Section. Ambulance collected horse at STRAZEELE left by SOUTH IRISH HORSE. O.C. Relieves Section horses to go to proceed to STRAZEELE. Marched 50 To Kennels of 50 INFANTRY BDE. 8 horses & mule admitted to Section. O.C. Inspecting hallured horses	
"	"	16		
"	"	17	O.C. 2 NCO's and 2 Men proceed to CAESTRE Station. Horses to 13 Veterinary Hospital 16 horses. 14 horses admitted to Section. O.C. Inspecting hallured horses	

Army Form C. 2118.

WAR DIARY
or
INTELLIGENCE SUMMARY.
(Erase heading not required.)

Place	Date	Hour	Summary of Events and Information	Remarks and references to Appendices
CAESTRE	Nov. 17		O.C. 2 N.C.O.'s & Men proceeded to CAESTRE station to entrain 16 horses to 13 Veterinary Hospital. 1 N.C.O. & Man as Conducting party. O.C. Inspected Picketed horses. 4 horses admitted to Section	
"	" 18		7 horses admitted to Section. Ambulance proceeded to HAZEBROUCK & conveyed horses from No.12. ANTI-AIR-CRAFT SECTION.	
"	" 19		4 horses admitted to Section. 2 horses destroyed. O.C. Inspected Remaining 50% of Animals of 50TH INFANTRY Bde.	
"	" 20		O.C. 2 N.C.O.'s & Men to CAESTRE Station to entrain 23 horses to 13 Veterinary Hospital. 1 N.C.O. & Men as Conducting party. Ambulance proceeded to STRAZEELE to convey horses from 147 Co A.S.C. O.C. Inspected Picketed horses.	

WAR DIARY
or
INTELLIGENCE SUMMARY
(Erase heading not required.)

Army Form C. 2118.

Place	Date	Hour	Summary of Events and Information	Remarks and references to Appendices
BABSTRE	Mch 21		1. N.C.O. then proceeded to NIEPPE as advance party to take over billets there from No. 33. Mobile Veterinary Section	
CAESTRE – NIEPPE	22		Section fitted up having cleaned up. Rest proceeded from to NIEPPE. During the short rest at CAESTRE the weather was fine & tried full opportunity was taken to give the Section a thorough overhauling. The Section was put through mounted rheometer drill & N.C.O's & other small parties were sent to various places to erect ingenious horses shelters & field kennels etc. The horse ford was despatched in advance of Section. It Collecting Supplies (forage en route). The Section having evacuated of horses to 13 Veterinary hospital proceeded at its own pace not being hampered with transport to NIEPPE & got the Section of its transport	

WAR DIARY
or
INTELLIGENCE SUMMARY.
(Erase heading not required.)

Army Form C. 2118.

Place	Date	Hour	Summary of Events and Information	Remarks and references to Appendices
NIEPPE	23		Fine morning before lunch, was good by the day was very bad but not too bad. On hand 7 horses unserviceable. 1 N.C.O. & 1 man as Con ducting party. 4 horses left by 33 battle Veterinary section.	
			Rules & horse standings duty, a great accumulation of manure & Section was busy cleaning up. 2 horses admitted.	
"	24		1 horse admitted	
"	25		O.C. 2 N.C.O's & 1 man to STEENWERCK Station to entrain 13 Veterinary Hospital 4 horses Ambulance conveying one horse. She finished at this station here the heat het ret by the station.	
			7 horses & 2 mules admitted. Section.	
"	26		2 horses admitted by Section	
"	27		O.C. 2 N.C.O's & 8 men proceeded to STEENWERCK Station to entrain 11 horses & mules 173 Veterinary Hospital. 1 N.C.O. & 1 man as Conducting party.	

WAR DIARY
or
INTELLIGENCE SUMMARY.
(Erase heading not required.)

Army Form C. 2118.

Place	Date	Hour	Summary of Events and Information	Remarks and references to Appendices
NIEPPE	March 28		2 horses & 3 mules admitted.	
"	" 29		Reinforcements to Joined Section.	
"	" 30		2 horses admitted.	
"	" 31		6 horses admitted. 1 destroyed.	
			2 horses & 1 mule admitted.	
			O.C. bought horses at 17 Divisional Train all the	
			Staff of horses. O.C. took our Veterinary charge of	
			the Divisional Train.	

J.F. Kennel Cranlane
O.C. 29 Mobile Vet. Sec.

Army Form C. 2118.

WAR DIARY
or
INTELLIGENCE SUMMARY.
(Erase heading not required.)

29 Mobile Veterinary Section 17 Division April 1916.

Place	Date	Hour	Summary of Events and Information	Remarks and references to Appendices
NIEPPE.	April 1.		O.C. 2 N.C.O.s and 10 men proceeded to STEENWERCK Station to entrain 13 horses & 2 mules to No. 13. Veterinary Hospital. 1 N.C.O. & 7 men as conducting party. Ambulance conveyed one horse. 3 horses admitted to Section. O.C. received S.A.D. horses at 116. Co. A.S.C.	
"	2		7 horses admitted to Section. O.C. Inspected horses at 116. Co. A.S.C. and Mullines doubtful case at 118. Co. A.S.C.	
"	3		11 horses & 1 mule admitted to Section. O.C. Inspected Mullines horses.	
"	4		O.C. 2 N.C.O.s and 11 men proceeded to STEENWERCK Station to entrain 17 horses & 1 mule to 13 Veterinary Hospital. 1 N.C.O. & 9 men as conducting party. 2 horses admitted to Section. N.C.O.S. Kit had an accident & carried on at H.Q. Office of A.D.V.S. Inspected Mullines horses.	

J.F. Knott
Capt.

WAR DIARY
INTELLIGENCE SUMMARY

Army Form C. 2118.

29 Mobile Section
April 1916.

Place	Date	Hour	Summary of Events and Information	Remarks and references to Appendices
NIEPPE.	April 5		O.C. Inspected 13 Riding horses at C.R.A. Passed fit to go to AMMO. parks.	
"	6		2 horses & 1 mule admitted to section. Inspecting Mules horses at C.R.A. at H.Q. afternoon.	
"	7		1 mule admitted to section. Inspected horses C.R.A. horses – no reactors. R.A.V.S. visited Section at H.Q.	
"	8		O.C. 3 N.C.O's and 10 men proceed to STEENWERCK to take 8 horses & 3 mules to 13 Veterinary Hospital. Also 5 men as conducting party. Horses & 1 mule admitted to section.	
"	9		2 horse admitted to Section. Ambulance conveying one horse from 146. Co A.S.C. broken up mile.	
"	10		3 horse admitted to Section	
"	11		2 horse admitted to Section	

J.P. Kurulane

Army Form C. 2118.

29 Mobile Section
April 1916

WAR DIARY
or
INTELLIGENCE SUMMARY.
(Erase heading not required.)

Place	Date	Hour	Summary of Events and Information	Remarks and references to Appendices
NIEPPE	April 12		O.C. 2 NCO's and 11 men proceeded to STEENWERCK to obtain 12 horses & 1 mule to 13 Veterinary Hospital. 1 N.C.O and 2 men as escort sling carts. 3 horses & 1 mule admitted. Which proved too weak or lame for use anywhere	
"	13		O.C. 1 N.C.O visited mules left by 13 Royal Scots. 34 Division at farm of Mr HERNU of NIEPPE. This mule was evacuated 19 sheld[?] evans[?] received from Remounts	
"	14		1 Horse admitted Hospital	
"	15		10 horses admitted Hospital	
"	16		O.C. 2 NCO's and 4 men proceeded to STEENWERCK Station to obtain horses for 13 Veterinary Hospital. Horses & mules N.C.O. as orderly along routes.	

J.R.[?] signature

WAR DIARY
or
INTELLIGENCE SUMMARY.

Army Form C. 2118.

29 Mobile Section
April 1916

Place	Date	Hour	Summary of Events and Information	Remarks and references to Appendices
NIEPPE	April 17		2 horse 1 mule arrived h.Q. 8k.m. 87 had colic in the a.m. from Pimento. Ambulance sent to Advance Workshops BAILLEUL for Repairs returned to S1 whilst there Spare parts for Shafts which for this was inexperienced.	
"	"	18	4 horse arrived to Section	
"	"	19	7 horse arrived to Section	
"	"	20	3 horse admitted to Section. Enemy shelling nightmare had 1 Camp in their effort to destroy the big gun in next field all of the horses had to be removed to a place farther for 2 hours	
"	"	21	1 horse admitted to Section	
"	"	22	O.C. 2 N.O.O.F.8 Men proceeded to STEENWERCK Anker Section	PR Kirula

WAR DIARY or INTELLIGENCE SUMMARY

Army Form C. 2118.

2 Mobile Section
April 5.

Place	Date	Hour	Summary of Events and Information	Remarks and references to Appendices
NIEPPE	April 22	10 hrs	to 13 Motorized Workshop. 14.00 2 n.c.o's from no 4 and n.c.o's 4 party.	
"	23		O.C. 2 n.c.o. & 18 men proceed to STEENWERCK to obtain 39 Remounts	
			for Division. 4 horses admitted to Section from Remounts. 5 other horses admitted from Units.	
"	24		3 horses admitted to Section. 1 animal admitted with dead up nail destroyed.	
"	25		5 horses 1 mule admitted to Section.	
"	27		1 horse admitted to Section. Took over duties of A.D.V.S. while	
			Major W.W.K. Neale was on leave of absence.	
			In evening had to evacuate premises being all Labor	
			and Sick horses to a place of safety owing to the	
			close proximity of Enemy Heavy Shells.	

J.P. Stewart
Capt.

WAR DIARY
or
INTELLIGENCE SUMMARY.

Army Form C. 2118.

29 Mobile Section
April 1916

Place	Date	Hour	Summary of Events and Information	Remarks and references to Appendices
NIEPPE	April 28		At 2 P.M. every shed & pen were very close to billets and animals had to be taken away to a place of safety. Owing to some of the animals being very lame it was a slow proceeding. Three standings of shelter freely covered not large piece of high Inflamme Shell fragments. My animals had not been so she only moved on but several casualties would have resulted to them horses. At 6th Division Horse not badly returns for D.A.V.S. Second Army. 5 horses admitted Kitchen	
"	29		O.C. 2 N Co's & Hen proceeded to STEENWERCK taking 14 horses to 13 Veterinary Hospital. 1 N.C.O. & 1 man as conducting party 7 horses to W. aelle admitted Kitchen all out Ruphelhound	

J.P. Kinnaird Capt.

XVI

2 Mobile Section
April 1916

Vol 10

WAR DIARY
or
INTELLIGENCE SUMMARY.
(Erase heading not required.)

Army Form C. 2118.

7

Place	Date	Hour	Summary of Events and Information	Remarks and references to Appendixes
DIEPPE	April 29		at offices of N.C.Os. for Autres Ferrieres afternoon.	
"	" 30		I was admitted to action. At 1.00 PM N.C.O of guard gave the alarm for enemy T.B. attack. Section paraded in a O.C. and "stood to" for 1 hour a no sign of the appearing & reports from refuging huts that he has to go on or or from the section put out + the owners there had time to be ready at a moments notice at 2.0 Church morning for Autres Ferrieres.	

JV Kinnel
Capt.
O.C. 29 M.V.S

Vol 11
XVII

Army Form C. 2118.

29. Mobile Veterinary Section.

May. 1916.

WAR DIARY
or
INTELLIGENCE SUMMARY.
(Erase heading not required.)

Place	Date	Hour	Summary of Events and Information	Remarks and references to Appendices
NIEPPE	1		OC 2N.C.O's and 10 men proceeded to Steenwerck Station to entrain horses to horse to No. 13 VETERINARY HOSPITAL. 1 NCO and 1 man as conducting party. 1 horse admitted to sick lines as suffering from debility of anus.	
"	2		5 horses admitted to Section. 5 men inoculated with new Vaccine for Typhoid. At Office parades for duties there.	
"	3		At office parades, horsing & at H.Q. "D" Office. At 2 pm enemy started to bombard Jun horizon men billets. Horses and men being in danger - moved the section along with sick horses to a place of safety along the NIEPPE-ARMENTIERES Railway lines & was temporary lines. At 8 pm the enemy ceased firing when horses returned to billets - horses being kept to open field and not in stables as before.	

Army Form C. 2118.

WAR DIARY
or
INTELLIGENCE SUMMARY.

(Erase heading not required.)

29 Mobile Veterinary Section

May 1916

2

Place	Date	Hour	Summary of Events and Information	Remarks and references to Appendices
MEPPE.	3		At 10 P.M. the enemy again opened fire when all horses were brought back to temporary lines and brought to front then back after some little time as enemy again commenced fire. Attending to duties & Duties provisioning.	
"	4		7 am enemy again shelled our position with 8" shells and men and animals were brought away to temporary lines which had been got ready for an intended stay. At 10 am every cannon fire to them same again at 12 noon this being kept up for some time. All horses pushed out & new road shelters near them. Attending to duties of ADVS and evacuated 7 horses and 2 mules for No.813 VETERINARY HOSPITAL from STEENWERCK Station. 1 N.C.O. + 1 man as conducting party.	

T2134. Wt. W708—776. 500000. 4/16. Str J. C. & S.

WAR DIARY
or
INTELLIGENCE SUMMARY.

Army Form C. 2118.

2 Mobile Vety Sect

May 1916

(Erase heading not required.)

Place	Date	Hour	Summary of Events and Information	Remarks and references to Appendices
NIEPPE	5		Men horses turned out at 8.P.M. The alarm sounded, then fell in till the Lebels stood to at 10 P.M. Orders received when men returned to their Beds but were to turn out at a moments notice. Morning at Office parades	
"	6		Day passed quietly — still occupying temporary lines at Office parades kept up to V.O's Return.	
"	7		A.D.V.S returned off leave when I handed over duties parades.	
"	8		35 horses admitted to section. D.D.V.R 2nd Army inspected at Section horses from the Division for casting.	

9/P.K.

Army Form C. 2118.

WAR DIARY
or
INTELLIGENCE SUMMARY. 29 Mobile Vety Section

May 1916

(Erase heading not required.)

Place	Date	Hour	Summary of Events and Information	Remarks and references to Appendices
NIEPPE	9		O.C. 2 NCO's & 12 men proceeded to STEENWERCK Station to entrain 33 horses and 5 mules to NO. 13. VETERINARY HOSPITAL. 1 N.C.O & men as conducting party. The Ambulance conveyed one bad case. 1 horse admitted to Section	
"	10		Ambulance collected animal from YORK DRAGOONS. 3 horses admitted to Section.	
"	11		Ambulance proceed to YORKS LANCS. transport lines to BIZET to collect 1 wounded mule. 44 horses admitted to Section punctually MANGE cases.	
"	12		O.C. 2 N.C.O's and 14 men proceeded to STEENWERCK Station to entrain 42 horses & 6 mules to NO. 13. VETERINARY HOSPITAL. 1 N.C.O. and 6 men as conducting party.	

99 R H

WAR DIARY or INTELLIGENCE SUMMARY

Army Form C. 2118.

29 Mobile Vety Section

May 1916

Place	Date	Hour	Summary of Events and Information	Remarks and references to Appendices
NIEPPE.	12		9 horses destroyed in Section. O.C. holding enquiry with N.C.O. in charge - negative result for close examination of wound cavity being done a polypus was found.	
"	13		1	
"	14		2 horses admitted to Section.	
"	15		5 horses admitted to Section.	
"	16		5 horses admitted to Section. O.C. in c/o of 10 men proceeded to STEENWERCK Station to entrain 13 horses + 1 mule for no. 13 VETERINARY HOSPITAL. 1 N.C.O. and 1 man as conducting party.	

WBK

WAR DIARY or INTELLIGENCE SUMMARY

Army Form C. 2118.

29. Mobile Vety Section

May 1916

Place	Date	Hour	Summary of Events and Information	Remarks and references to Appendices
NIEPPE	17		5 horses & mules admitted to section.	
"	18		2 horses admitted to section.	
" - LA MOTTE	19	9.30am	Lined up to hand over 18 mules at 9. a.m for Rest Area. Men having been issued with Haversite into Trucks & picking gear to start to rail. 9.S. Buffum proceeded to Supply dump to draw 2 days rations for 17 NCO & Men and horsed complete via STEENWERCK where 10 horses & 1 mule were entrained for 13 VETERINARY HOSPITAL. 1 N.C.O. and 1 man as conducting party.	
		10am	Section proceeded via MOTTE BOOM to Vieux BERQUIN through the FORET DE NIEPPE to LA MOTTE Section billeting on HAZEBROUCK Road. The trek was good & nothing occurred while on the march. Fine day.	

J.P.K.

WAR DIARY or INTELLIGENCE SUMMARY

Army Form C. 2118.

J. Mulet's Ind Sec...

Place	Date	Hour	Summary of Events and Information	Remarks and references to Appendices
NIEPPE – LAMOTTE	19.		Was extremely hot but transport animals found little difficulty in pulling their loads. The roads were in good condition. Billet was reached 4 P.M.	
LAMOTTE – TILQUES.	20.	At 8.30 a.m	Section proceeded on its line of March – no casualties having occurred nor men favourite etc. Route was by WALLON CAPPEL – EBBLINCHEM – RENESCURE – ARQUES – ST OMER to TILQUES. The day was again very hot, but dusty. Teams about half were hard trot. Transport animals. No better off – Section halted & fed on RENESCURE. The hour of arrival is good time, nothing coming to hand that sock. men were had trot Arrived at TILQUES 4 P.M.	
TILQUES	21		Hutting & Stables were built &c.	

J.S.Simon

Army Form C. 2118.

WAR DIARY
or
INTELLIGENCE SUMMARY.

99 Mobile Vety Section
May 1916

(Erase heading not required.)

Place	Date	Hour	Summary of Events and Information	Remarks and references to Appendices
FIQUES	22		Sent return of Officers, Cart horses &c held built for non truce combatants & proceeded on leave of absence to ENGLAND IRELAND.	
	22-31		On Leave fortune.	

J. Skinnel A.V.C.
Capt & a/c
OC. 99 Mt. vet. Sec.
1/6

WAR DIARY or INTELLIGENCE SUMMARY

Army Form C. 2118.

June 29 Mobile Veterinary Vol 12 Section

Place	Date	Hour	Summary of Events and Information	Remarks and references to Appendices
TILQUES	June 1		Arrived (OC) NB Leave Ross over Command of Section from the address who had been acting.	
"	"	2	2 horses admitted to Section	
"	"	2	42 animals admitted to Section all mange from 20 Bde R.F.A. O.C. 2 N.C.O's and 12 men proceeded to WATTEN Station to entrain 56 animals for No. 13 Veterinary Hospital. 1 N.C.O and 6 men as convoy etc 9 party	
"	"	3	5 animals admitted to Section	
"	"	4	"	
"	"	5	4 "	
"	"	6	O.C. 2 N.C.O's and 9 men proceeded to entrain 20 horses for No. 13 Veterinary Hospital. 1 N.C.O and 3 men as convoy etc party. Ambulance convoyed 1 case to Section from 8 =½ BRIDGING TRAIN. CLAIRMARAIS. ST. OMER	
"	"	7	7 animals admitted to Section	

Army Form C. 2118.

29 Mobile Veterinary Section

WAR DIARY
or
INTELLIGENCE SUMMARY.

(Erase heading not required.)

Place	Date	Hour	Summary of Events and Information	Remarks and references to Appendices
THIEVES	June 8		4 Animals admitted to Section.	
"	"	9	O.C. 2 N.C.O's and 8 men proceeded to ST OMER Station to entrain horses. 1 N.C.O 12 men as conducting party	
"	"	10	15 horses admitted to Section	
"	"	11	Ambulance proceeded to ST OMER at hour over 2 sick cases to No.13 Veterinary Section 1/c 2 etailes St Omer for evacuation to No.13 Veterinary Hospital O.C. 1 N.C.O and 4 men conveying 9 60 other horses animals were left at 9 am at Section two entrained 9 for 4th ARMY next day.	
"	"	12	Left Riflets for STATION. ST. OMER at 8 AM arriving 9 AM and immediately proceeded to entrain the Section complete, horses having been first watered. Train moved off at 12 noon for LONGEAU via ABBEVILLE at ABBEVILLE arrived at 6 P.M	WK

A 2353 W.t. W 2544/1454 700,000 5/15 D D & L. A.D.S.S./Forms/C. 2118.

Army Form C. 2118.

99 Mobile Veterinary Section

WAR DIARY
or
INTELLIGENCE SUMMARY.
(Erase heading not required.)

Instructions regarding War Diaries and Intelligence Summaries are contained in F. S. Regs., Part II and the Staff Manual respectively. Title pages will be prepared in manuscript.

Place	Date	Hour	Summary of Events and Information	Remarks and references to Appendices
TRAVES — ST.OMER — ALLONVILLE	June 12		Where a half-hour halt was made. to water Mules horses & let them tea. at 6.30 p.m. moved off to LONGEAU arriving there 9-30 P.M. Vets mus a d horsed to ALLONVILLE via AMIENS arriving at ALLONVILLE 2-30 A.M. having had a very hot night from St Section arrived without a single casualty.	
ALLONVILLE	" 13		Repaired sheds for men & horse lines. 1 mule admitted.	
"	" 14		1 horse admitted. The clerks who advanced 1 horse at 11 P.M.	99 M
"	" 15		—	
"	" 16		1 horse admitted	
"	" 17		2 horses 1 mule admitted	
"	" 18		—	
"	" 19		Ambulance proceeded to LONGEAU to convey animal	9 M

Army Form C. 2118.

WAR DIARY
or
INTELLIGENCE SUMMARY.

29 Mobile Veterinary Section

(Erase heading not required.)

Place	Date	Hour	Summary of Events and Information	Remarks and references to Appendices
ALLONVILLE	June 19		A section. 4 horses admitted. 1 discharged cured. Section Routine.	
"	" 20		"	
"	" 21		O.C. 2 N.C.Os. 7 men ambulance proceeded to FRECHENCOURT to entrain 6 horses for No. 7 Veterinary Hospital. 1 N.C.O as conducting party.	
"	" 22		1 horse admitted.	
"	" 23		O.C. 1 N.C.O 4 horse mes to 63 Div Ambulance, to Spare hold Glisenum Suspecto 18 mules 40 horses as large cases noted.	
"	" 24		1 horse admitted to be shot	
"	" 25		1 horse " "	
"	" 26		1 horse admitted. 1 horse dis charged.	
"	" 27		O.C. 1 N.C.O. 6 men proceeded to FRECH IN COURT to entrain 6 horses to No. 7 Veterinary Hospital. 1 N.C.O as conducting party.	MK

Army Form C. 2118.

WAR DIARY
or
INTELLIGENCE SUMMARY.

29 Mobile Veterinary Section

(Erase heading not required.)

Instructions regarding War Diaries and Intelligence Summaries are contained in F. S. Regs., Part II. and the Staff Manual respectively. Title pages will be prepared in manuscript.

Place	Date	Hour	Summary of Events and Information	Remarks and references to Appendices
ACHONVILLE MERICOURT	June 28.		Section moved complete from ACHONVILLE to MERICOURT at 1-30 PM arriving 4-30 PM where the Section bivouced at with NO 12 Mobile Veterinary Section for the night and Stood to' awaiting orders for advance after fighting troops who had the day. Standing to.	
MERICOURT "	29. 30		Standing to, making further arrangements for the "move forward".	

J J Stennel
Capt S
O.C. 29 M.V.S
30/6/16
S. F. F. field

17 July
29 M.V.S.
Vol 13

Confidential
WAR DIARY
29 M.T. Vet Section
17th Divn
July 1/31st 1916

Army Form C. 2118.

WAR DIARY
or
INTELLIGENCE SUMMARY.
(Erase heading not required.)

29 Mobile Veterinary Section

July 1916.

Instructions regarding War Diaries and Intelligence Summaries are contained in F. S. Regs., Part II. and the Staff Manual respectively. Title pages will be prepared in manuscript.

Place	Date	Hour	Summary of Events and Information	Remarks and references to Appendices
MERICOURT	July 1.		At MERICOURT Railway Station. Standing to. Received Arrival of a G.S. Waggon to enable Section Lorry into forage for "move forward."	
"	" 2		Standing to at MERICOURT.	
"	3		Standing to at MERICOURT.	
MERICOURT — RIBEMONT.	4	3.	Moved from MERICOURT to RIBEMONT and took over from Mobile Section 21st Division. On arrival Heaps of Horse manure found having been Concealed. O.C. proceeded with 2 N.C.O's and 5 Men to DERNACOURT and held a Collecting Post at E.20.2.3 Sheet 62D NE. I. N.C.O and 4 men hire M/T in provision of Post.	
RIBEMONT.	"		Ambulance first proceeded to MENURTE to convey around from Casualty lines to West Forks and late proceeded to BAZZE to	

Army Form C. 2118.

WAR DIARY
or
INTELLIGENCE SUMMARY.

29 Mobile Veterinary Section

July 1916.

(Erase heading not required.)

Instructions regarding War Diaries and Intelligence Summaries are contained in F. S. Regs., Part II. and the Staff Manual respectively. Title pages will be prepared in manuscript.

Place	Date	Hour	Summary of Events and Information	Remarks and references to Appendices
BEMONT.	July 4.		Collected animal from St. Hopkins Gun Co. 4 animals admitted to Section.	
"	5.		OC visited Collecting Post and inspected animals received from units.	
"	6		Animal belonging to 10 West Yorks. destroyed in Section. 4 horses and 1 mule admitted to Section	
"	7		OC visited Collecting Post. Section Routine.	
"	8		Section Routine.	
"	9		OC visited Collecting Post and sent 4 animals into Section. Animals are coming in.	
"	10		9 animals evacuated to No. 9 VETERINARY HOSPITAL from MERICOURT. Train conducting party being provided from The Base AVC. 13 animals rcvd.	
"	#10		3 animals were received for Section on 11-7-16. Advance post known to CAVILLON on 11-7-16. Advance post was taken in and Section got animals ready for evacuation	

Army Form C. 2118.

WAR DIARY
or
INTELLIGENCE SUMMARY.

(Erase heading not required.)

29 Motor Veterinary Section

July 1916

Place	Date	Hour	Summary of Events and Information	Remarks and references to Appendices
RIBEMONT.	11		33 Animals evacuated to NO.7. VETERINARY HOSPITAL. Conducting parties being provided by A.V.C. Base Units. Unit was handed over to N0.33. to B.V.E. VETERINARY SECTION when section proceeded on line of march to CAVILLON. Roots being by HEILLY, LA HOUSSOYE, QUERRIEU where horses were watered and fed. Menu through AMIENS to PICQUIGNY to Billet at BOIS DE CAVILLON. The march was made in very good time and kits were soon unpacked, men fed, horses fed, no casualties. Horse lines laid down, billets got ready for inspection of O.C.	
CAVILLON			
CAVILLON.	12	at midnight 51 MACHINE GUN CORPS came into and occupied Billet and owing to error of .... of Billet the Motor Section had to turn out. A .... the .... to CAVILLON. These .... were laid and motor .... ready to receive O.C. IN C.O and 4 men billets a	

T2134. Wt. W708–776. 500000. 4/15. Str J. C. & S.

WAR DIARY
or
INTELLIGENCE SUMMARY

Army Form C. 2118.

29 Mobile Veterinary Section

July 1916

Place	Date	Hour	Summary of Events and Information	Remarks and references to Appendices
CAVILLON	12		Left by other Animals at MOLLIENS-VIDAMES, OREVIL, OISSY, RIENCOURT, LE MESGES and SOUES. 8 Animals attached.	
"	13		O.C. visited St PIERRE à COVY and MOLLIENS-VIDAMES & Collect 2 horses left by 15 Bde RFA and 2/ MIDDLESEX Regt. 3 Animals admitted to Section	
"	14		Section Routine. O.C. visited RIENCOURT and MONTON-VILLERS to collect 8 horses left by the 21 Divison and Cheshire Field Co. RE.	
"	15		Section moved from CAVILLON to PONT RENY. En Route 7 Animals were evacuated to NO.14 VETERINARY HOSPITAL from VIGNACOURT Station. Owing to position of VIGNACOURT being in opposite direction to PONT-RENY an extra 20 mile had to be marched. Sick Animals were sent away in early morning. Section proceeding later to P.O.RVIGNY where the bun proceed of letter with transport. Meanwhile OC with a duty proceeded to VIGNACOURT	

Army Form C. 2118.

WAR DIARY
or
INTELLIGENCE SUMMARY.
(Erase heading not required.)

39 Mobile Veterinary Section

Feb / 1916.

Place	Date	Hour	Summary of Events and Information	Remarks and references to Appendices
CAVILLON – PONT-REMY	15.		Due to evacuation of animals and being back heavy to PICQUIGNY. At 3 PM Section resumed march to PONT-REMY arriving at 6 PM after a long march. Section killed one horse cast out for Rupture of animator.	
PONT REMY.	16.		Section Routine	
"	17.		7 Animals admitted to Section. O.C. visited L'ETOILE and FLEXICOURT to collect 3 animals left by 115 Battery R.F.A. & A Battery R.F.A.	
"	18.		8 Animals evacuated to NO. 22. VETERINARY. HOSPITAL. Section Routine	
"	19.		Section Routine	
"	20.		Section Routine	
"	21.		Section Routine	
"	22.		Section proceeded to RIBEMONT in a two day march. The first day being from PONT REMY to RAINNEVILLE and second day RAINNEVILLE to RIBEMONT. Section moved in	

WAR DIARY
or
INTELLIGENCE SUMMARY

Army Form C. 2118.

29 Mobile Veterinary Section
July 1916

Place	Date	Hour	Summary of Events and Information	Remarks and references to Appendices
RIBEMONT	22		Had without any incident to report. Section evacuating sick	
"	23		horses without room for sick horses. 39 former sick	
			horses occupied by a Company of Infantry and another	
			had no use for horse standings. These have been	
			over by arrangement.	
"	24		Section Routine	
"	25		Ambulance proceeded to 79 Bde R.F.A. to convey animal	
			to Section. 16 horses and 2 mules admitted to Section.	
"	26		27 Animals evacuated from MERICOURT. Hire conducted had	
			being provided from Base. 37 horses and 1 mule admitted	
			to Section	
"	27		37 horses and 1 mule evacuated from MERICOURT	
"	28		19 horses and 2 mules admitted to Section	
"	29		4 horses and 1 mule admitted to Section	

W.P. Hurrell

WAR DIARY
or
INTELLIGENCE SUMMARY.
(Erase heading not required.)

Army Form C. 2118.

29 Mobile Veterinary Section
July 1916

Place	Date	Hour	Summary of Events and Information	Remarks and references to Appendices
REBEMONT	30		16 horses and 3 mules evacuated from MERICOURT to No 7 VETERINARY HOSPITAL. Ambulance proceeded to B/178 RFA picking up Animals to Section – 4 horses & 3 mules admitted to Section.	
"	31		16 Animals evacuated from MERICOURT to No 7 VETERINARY Section. HOSPITAL — 4 were admitted to Section. The horse Ambulance MSC for the Inns Corps during has proved on invaluable help of relieving the pressure on the Mobile Section as all the personnel was available to deal with the large numbers of animals that were admitted the vast majority of which required clipping. Upon owing to the movements of the Inns Guns great movements have been during been caused of Section personnel were ordered to the Inns looking after the horses on the lines, more than with [?] harness, the harness on the turn over mages	

Army Form C. 2118.

29 Mobile Veterinary Section

July 1916

WAR DIARY
or
INTELLIGENCE SUMMARY.
(Erase heading not required.)

Place	Date	Hour	Summary of Events and Information	Remarks and references to Appendices
Beaumont	31		Parties from the Bn. to continue to work as for the good of the service as Mobile Sections long left complete more work could be got though and individual care bestowed on all animals no matter how great the rush hard Cavalry Stations could be established without the men prior to being suitably worked.	

P Stunkel Capt
O.C. 29 Mobile Vety Section

AUGUST 1916

WAR DIARY OF 29 MOBILE VETERINARY SECTION

Army Form C. 2118.

INTELLIGENCE SUMMARY

vol 13

Place	Date	Hour	Summary of Events and Information	Remarks and references to Appendices
RIBEMONT	1 August		Six horses & one Mule admitted to Section, one horse discharged cured. Ambulance proceeded to DERNANCOURT to 79 Brigade RFA to collect wounded horse, later Ambulance 17 DAC at EDGE HILL siding to convey animal to Section, took over 64 Head Collars at MERICOURT.	
"	2		XV Corps Ambulance sent to A Ordnance workshop for repairs, one horse admitted to Section, one horse discharged. (to 1899).	
"	3		O.C. 2 N.C.O's proceeded to MERICOURT to evacuate 7 horses & 2 mules to No 7 VETERINARY HOSPITAL, train conducting party being provided by Base details. At 5 a.m. O.C. proceeded to ALBERT to erect Advanced Collecting Pool, 1 Sergeant & 4 men (mounted) being the personnel. E 11. d 6. 8. Sheet 62D N.E. Map reference of Collecting Pool	

AUGUST 1916

WAR DIARY 29 MOBILE VETERINARY SECTION

Army Form C. 2118.

INTELLIGENCE SUMMARY

Place	Date	Hour	Summary of Events and Information	Remarks and references to Appendices
RIBEMONT	4 August		O.C. visited following food and arranged for evacuation of sick & wounded horses to Section. 22 horses & 6 mules being admitted. Owing to Railway accident at MERICOURT Station the previous day, 8 animals that were being sent down to Base, were returned to Section and another truck was obtained & the animals were sent down to the Base. The accident was due to wagon shunting, the bottom of the truck being pulled out & animals were most fortunate to escape with only skin abrasions.	
"	5		Section Routine	
"	6		O.C. 2 N.C.O's & 9 men proceeded to MERICOURT Station to evacuate 26 horses & 3 mules to No. 7 VETERINARY HOSPITAL, train conducting party being provided by Base details	

T2134. Wt. W708—776. 500000. 4/16. Sir J.C. & S.

AUGUST 1916

WAR DIARY 29 Mobile Veterinary Section Army Form C. 2118.

INTELLIGENCE SUMMARY

Place	Date	Hour	Summary of Events and Information	Remarks and references to Appendices
RIBEMONT	7 August		5 Horses and 2 mules admitted sick from Advanced Collecting Post.	
"	8		15 Horses and 1 mule received from collecting post. Civilian Horse was diseased by O.C. for a deep wound result of a bayonet accident.	
	9		Section Routine.	
	10		That proceeded to 17 Divisional Ammn. Col. at ALBERT to collect 1 mule. O.C. 2 N.C.O's & 8 men proceeded to MERICOURT Station to evacuate to No 4 VETERINARY HOSPITAL 23 Horses & 5 mules. Conducting party being provided by Base details.	J.S. Rohhely Capt

T2134. Wt. W708—776. 500000. 4/15. Sir J. C. & S.

AUGUST 1916

WAR DIARY

29 MOBILE VETERINARY SECTION

Army Form C. 2118.

INTELLIGENCE SUMMARY

Place	Date	Hour	Summary of Events and Information	Remarks and references to Appendices
RIBEMONT	11 August		7 Horses and 2 mules brought in from Collecting Post. 1 mule being conveyed in by Ambulance. 1 Horse admitted to Section	
	12		9 Horses & 3 mules brought in from Collecting Post. Ambulance conveying 1 wounded Horse.	
	13		O.C. 2 N.C.Os & 5 men proceeded to MERICOURT Station to evacuate to No 7. VETERINARY HOSPITAL 17 horses and 5 mules. 1 N.C.O. & 2 men proceeding conveying party Base details having been withdrawn, Section having to provide its own party. Collecting Post withdrawn as No 26 MOBILE VETERINARY SECTION, 14 DIVISION, came as relief. Accommodation was found in Section for men and	

AUGUST, 1916

WAR DIARY
of 29 MOBILE VETERINARY SECTION
INTELLIGENCE SUMMARY

Army Form C. 2118.

Place	Date	Hour	Summary of Events and Information	Remarks and references to Appendices
RIBEMONT	13 Aug		Horses of 26 M.V.S. At MERICOURT Station the O.C. destroyed animal suffering from TETANUS. His animal was left by 4th Australian M.V.S. Party returning from Advanced Collecting Post brought in 10 Sections, 1 wounded horse and 2 mules.	
"	14	"	Section Routine.	
"	15		1 Animal admitted with Colic from 2/5 LANCASHIRE FUSILIERS. The driver states that the animal had colic previous 12 hours & that several stimulant and Physic balls had been given to it. The animal was dreadfully blown out & in great distress, an enema was applied & rectal examination made, when the intestines were found very tense & rectum contracted	

AUGUST 1916

WAR DIARY

29 MOBILE VETERINARY SECTION

INTELLIGENCE SUMMARY

Army Form C. 2118.

Place	Date	Hour	Summary of Events and Information	Remarks and references to Appendices
RIBEMONT	15th August		Here was a veluitis, but this was due to the administration of salt by some person to induce purging to state. 191 was decided to tap the animal which was done but in a very short time Average had slowed out again when a second of the tricars was investigated. A second internal animal examination was made & after a short internal animal exys as had as ever. Thinking some intestine obstruction was the cause of the Colic, eserine was given hypodermically. To get rid of obstruction. 1 half grain was administered & except for slight salivation nothing else was noticed from injection. Two further injections of half grain doses were given during the day. As this without result, next morning was given a grain of eserine without result & again tapped abdomen	J Spencer Lt

AUGUST, 1916

WAR DIARY
of 29 MOBILE VETERINARY SECTION
INTELLIGENCE SUMMARY

Army Form C. 2118.

Place	Date	Hour	Summary of Events and Information	Remarks and references to Appendices
RIBEMONT	15 Aug		Giving the case up as hopeless, and putting the animal out of its suffering, animal was destroyed, and a post mortem made, when the beginning of the small intestine was completely obstructed by a **DUNG BALL**. Also other DUNG BALLS were found. These dung balls varied in size from a small turnip to small potatoes, the two large dung balls weighed respectively 1lb 10oz & 1lb 10g in weight. They leaves one covering the obstruction? The nucleus for each dung ball was a small pebble.	
	16		2 horses & one mule admitted to Section	
	17		O.C. 1 N.C.O & 4 men proceeded to MERICOURT Station to evacuate 4 horses, 3 mules to No 9 VETERINARY HOSPITAL, 1 NCO in charge.	[signature]

AUGUST 1916

WAR DIARY of **29 MOBILE VETERINARY SECTION 8**

INTELLIGENCE SUMMARY.

Army Form C. 2118.

Place	Date	Hour	Summary of Events and Information	Remarks and references to Appendices
RIBEMONT	18 Aug		3 Animals admitted to Section	
"	19		O.C. 1 N.C.O. & 3 men collected 4 horses & 1 mule near ALBERT. Ambulance conveying 1 wounded animal	
"	20		O.C. 1 N.C.O. & 4 men proceeded to MERICOURT Station to evacuate 6 horses & 1 mule to No.7 VETERINARY HOSPITAL. O.C. 1 N.C.O. & 4 men collected 8 horses near BECORDEL	
"	21		O.C. 1 N.C.O. & 6 men proceeded to MERICOURT Station to evacuate 6 horses & 2 mules. 1 N.C.O. & an escorting party later Section marched the distance of 5 KILOMETRES to BONNAY where Artillery of 17 Division were concentrating. Section picketing in rear of D.A.C. Three animals admitted into Section viz: 2 horses & 1 mule	
RIBEMONT BONNAY.				

99 Kimberley Capt.

WAR DIARY
of 29 MOBILE VETERINARY SECTION
INTELLIGENCE SUMMARY

Army Form C. 2118.

AUGUST 1916

Place	Date	Hour	Summary of Events and Information	Remarks and references to Appendices
RIBEMONT	21 Aug		1 N.C.O + 2 men proceed to D.A.C. discharged as unsec. to D.A.C. 1 N.C.O + 2 men proceed to 26 M.V.S at RIBEMONT to evacuate 3 horses	
BONNAY				
BONNAY	22	12 noon	Section proceeded on line of march in rear of Divisional Artillery to RAINNEVILLE, where Section halted for that night. Yt march was through QUERRIEU, ALLONVILLE, CARDONETTE to RAINNEVILLE arriving at 3.30 p.m.	
RAINNEVILLE				
RAINNEVILLE	23	3/5	Section proceeded in rear of Artillery to OCCOCHES via COISY, BERTANGLES, FLESSELLES, HAVERNAS, CANAPLES, MONTRELET where Section watered & fed, thence to FIENVILLERS to AUTHIEUX to OCCOCHES arriving at midnight.	
OCCOCHES				

AUGUST 1916

Army Form C. 2118.

WAR DIARY
of 29 MOBILE VETERINARY SECTION
INTELLIGENCE SUMMARY.
(Erase heading not required.)

Instructions regarding War Diaries and Intelligence Summaries are contained in F.S. Regs., Part II. and the Staff Manual respectively. Title pages will be prepared in manuscript.

Place	Date	Hour	Summary of Events and Information	Remarks and references to Appendices
RAINNEVILLE OCCOCHES	23		When horses were put down & camp pitched. The march was a very long & tedious one, but animals arrived in good condition and men finished first.	
OCCOCHES GRINCOURT	24	12 noon	Section proceeded in rear of Artillery to new area arriving at 3.30 p.m. when duties of mobile section 56 D division was taken over. The march from RIBEMONT was a very long & tedious one, the weather was good & the roads in good marching condition. No casualties to men or horses. A few animals that had been sick were being LS playing up section for reason to waits. Four horses & 1 mule were left by outgoing M.V.S. These were taken over.	

W S Kendal Capt

AUGUST 1916

WAR DIARY of 29 MOBILE VETERINARY SECTION

Army Form C. 2118.

INTELLIGENCE SUMMARY.

Place	Date	Hour	Summary of Events and Information	Remarks and references to Appendices
GRINCOURT	25 Augt		Section Routine. Section busily engaged clearing up & preparing for reception of sick animals. 2 horses admitted sick.	
"	26	"	12 horses & 1 mule admitted sick	
"	27	"	1 mule left by 4 York & Lancs' Regt at BEAUMETZ was collected from MAIRE	
"	28	"	Section Routine & preparing standings for horses. C.R.E. VII Corps admitted Section Horse standings & took measurements etc., to erect horse standings at Corps Headquarters.	

J.P. Kenny Capt.

AUGUST 1916 WAR DIARY of 29 MOBILE VETERINARY SECTION

Army Form C. 2118.
INTELLIGENCE SUMMARY.
(Erase heading not required.)

Place	Date	Hour	Summary of Events and Information	Remarks and references to Appendices
GRINCOURT	29		Animal left by 117 Machine Gun Coy at HAUTE VISÉE north of DOUVRENS was collected by Ambulance float.	
			Arrived at Headquarters. 2 men proceeded to disinfecting purposes the walls & standings being thoroughly scrubbed & sealed with calcium sulphide solution	
			Some cases of mange were found amongst the civilian horses in this locality. Three horses received.	
"	30		O.C. 2 N.C.O. & 12 men proceeded to SAULTY-LARBRET to evacuate 25 horses & 2 mules to No.23 VETERINARY HOSPITAL. 1 N.C.O. & 3 men as conducting party. 2 horses admitted sick, 2 received.	9 [signature]

WAR DIARY

29 MOBILE VETERINARY SECTION

INTELLIGENCE SUMMARY

August 1916

Army Form C. 2118.

Instructions regarding War Diaries and Intelligence Summaries are contained in F.S. Regs., Part II. and the Staff Manual respectively. Title pages will be prepared in manuscript.

(Erase heading not required.)

Place	Date	Hour	Summary of Events and Information	Remarks and references to Appendices
GRINCOURT	31 August		Ambulance proceeded to B/282 5 Divisions collected horse. 5 Horses examined sick.	

J.P. Kennel
Capt. AVC
O.C. 29. Mob Vet Section

Confidential Vol 3

WAR DIARY
OF
29n Mob. Vet Section
SEPT. 1916

WAR DIARY or INTELLIGENCE SUMMARY

Army Form C. 2118.

2/9. Mobile Veterinary Section

September 1916

Place	Date	Hour	Summary of Events and Information	Remarks and references to Appendices
GRINCOURT	Sept.1		O.C. 2 N.C.O's and 9 men proceeded to MONDICOURT Station to entrain 12 horses and 1 mule to No.22. Veterinary Hospital.	
"	2		1 N.C.O. and 1 man as Conducting party. 17 horses and 3 mules admitted to Section.	
"	3		Ambulance proceeded to COOTERELLE to take home of 6 horses also admitted sick from LUCKNOW M.V.S. 3 horses and 1 mule evacuated to No.22. Veterinary Hospital O.C. 2 N.C.O.s and 10 men proceeded to MONDICOURT to entrain 23 horses and 1 mule to No.22. Veterinary Hospital.	
"	4		6 horses admitted sick lines.	
"	5		2 cases of mange evacuated to No.22. Veterinary Hospital wounded admitted sick.	
"	6		4 horses wounded to No.22. Veterinary Hospital.	
"	7		1 horse admitted sick. O.C. 2 N.C.O.s and 9 men proceeded	

Army Form C. 2118

WAR DIARY
or
INTELLIGENCE SUMMARY

29 Mobile Veterinary Section

(Erase heading not required.)

September 1916.

Instructions regarding War Diaries and Intelligence Summaries are contained in F. S. Regs., Part II. and the Staff Manual respectively. Title Pages will be prepared in manuscript.

Place	Date	Hour	Summary of Events and Information	Remarks and references to Appendices
RIACOURT	Sept. 7		to MONDICOURT to evacuate 10 horses and 1 mule to No. 22 Veterinary Hospital. Ambulance proceeded to P.A.S. to collect injured horse.	
"	8		5 horses evacuated from MONDICOURT Station to No. 22 Veterinary Hospital. 4 Animals admitted to sick lines	
"	9		8 horses evacuated to No. 22 Veterinary Station from MONDICOURT Station. 3 horses admitted sick	
"	10		9 horses and 1 mule admitted sick. D.D.V.S. III Army. Inspected Section.	
"	11		55 Animals admitted sick of which 3 were mules, one case of DEBILITY and were the Sudano cradled horses one to the "breaking up" of 80th Bde. R.F.A. on re-organization of Artillery Brigades	

1875 Wt. W593/826 1,000,000 4/15 J.B.C. & A. A.D.S.S./Forms/C. 2118.

Army Form C. 2118

WAR DIARY
or
INTELLIGENCE SUMMARY
(Erase heading not required.)

29. Mobile Veterinary Section

September 1916.

Place	Date	Hour	Summary of Events and Information	Remarks and references to Appendices
PINCOURT	Sept. 12		O.C. With section proceeded to SAULTY and had to evacuate 58 horses and 1 mule to No. 22 Veterinary Section. Cpl. FITZGERALD. B. A.V.C. the N.C.O i/c conducting party was detailed to remain at ABBEVILLE for course of instruction in Horse Clipping and Shortening of knives of STEWARTS CLIPPING MACHINE at NO. 5. VETERINARY. HOSPITAL. Ambulance proceeded to COVIN to collect sick & lame horses and bring to section for treatment. Animal was extensively injured to the foot as the nerves of a collision with an Engine. W.D. had lorry. Injuries were most unforeseen while and it was decided to destroy Animal and as this was done on 16/9/16 on authority from Remounts A.B.	
"	13		Animal of 146 Co. A.S.C. was destroyed by O.C. Animal was injured by collision with W.D. Motor lorry. Femur bone was fractured.	
"	14		7 horses evacuated to NO.22 Veterinary Hospital. 7 horses of trade admitted with influenza & a mare with foal.	

Army Form C. 2118

WAR DIARY
or
INTELLIGENCE SUMMARY

(Erase heading not required.)

29 Mobile Veterinary Section

September 1916

Place	Date	Hour	Summary of Events and Information	Remarks and references to Appendices
RINCOURT	Sept. 15		Evacuated remount foal to No. 22 Veterinary Hospital. 1 horse and 1 mule admitted sick.	
"	16		10 horses and 2 mules evacuated to No. 22 Veterinary Hospital from MONDICOURT. Ambulance proceeded to HENU to collect sick horse from Div. Amm. Col. Ambulance proceeded to PAS to collect sick horse from T.T. Cable Sect. R.E. Ambulance proceeded to WARLINCOURT to collect sick horse from 147 Co. A.S.C. 5 horses and 2 mules admitted sick.	
"	17			
"	18		10 horses and 2 mules evacuated from MONDICOURT Station to No. 22 Veterinary Hospital.	
"	19		Ambulance proceeded to MONDICOURT to collect sick horse from 52 Field Ambulance. 3 horses and 1 mule admitted sick	

J S Kinnaird

WAR DIARY or INTELLIGENCE SUMMARY

Army Form C. 2118

(Erase heading not required.)

Instructions regarding War Diaries and Intelligence Summaries are contained in F.S. Regs., Part II. and the Staff Manual respectively. Title Pages will be prepared in manuscript.

29. Mobile Veterinary Section

December 1916

Place	Date	Hour	Summary of Events and Information	Remarks and references to Appendices
RINCOURT	Sept 20		Ambulance proceeded to BAYENCOURT to collect sick animals left by unit on line of march. No. 614 Cat/Cch Sarks a/c was attached to take charge of number of sick animals for evacuation from Remount Yard. Sector FREVENT & No. 22 Veterinary Hospital.	
"	21	11 AM	14 horses and 2 mules evacuated from MONDICOURT station to No. 22 Veterinary Hospital. 5 horses and 2 mules admitted sick reserve.	
RINCOURT — E. MEILLARD	22		Section moved at 8. Am to proceed on line of march to Lining Area at St. RICQUIER. The move from G. RINCOURT was very sudden and as we were told to prepare and take winter quarters gear were now close to making stables, cook houses were sleeping huts etc. a great deal of breaking material had to be left and this we quickly utilized and section was almost complete when section had to leave. In moving to men to quarters an accumulation of rubbish had to be carted away as well as a seven accumulation of horse manure, clearing the horse lines was ??? a task it had to be begun some time	

WAR DIARY or INTELLIGENCE SUMMARY

Army Form C. 2118

Place	Date	Hour	Summary of Events and Information	Remarks and references to Appendices
RINCOURT LE MEILLARD	22.	9am	Chatsene + twist in Lines. At 9am section was ched out of billets to LE MEILLARD where the night was spent in bivouac. Roads was though MONDICOURT, DOULLENS, OCCOCHES. LE MEILLARD. The weather was fine and the roads in good order and were done in good time & all in good condition	
LE MEILLARD	23	9am	March was continued via BERNAVILLE; BEAUMETZ, CRAMONT COULONVILLERS & ST. RICQUIER arriving at Billets at DRUGY at 3.30 PM. Where was the last section got ready for reports of animals. The trees in close in very good two and furthers Crenaries. The weather being very fine & the roads good.	
ST. RICQUIER	24		Section Routine. 1 animal admitted sick	
"	25		OC Collected 1 horse & mule from BEAUVOIR from inhabitant animals being left by 17 D.A.C. also 1 mule from VILLIERS.L. Hospital left by 6. DORSET Regt. admitted sick. 4 horses 2 mules	

Army Form C. 2118

WAR DIARY
or
INTELLIGENCE SUMMARY
(Erase heading not required.)

29 Mobile Veterinary Section

September 1916

Instructions regarding War Diaries and Intelligence Summaries are contained in F.S. Regs., Part II. and the Staff Manual respectively. Title Pages will be prepared in manuscript.

Place	Date	Hour	Summary of Events and Information	Remarks and references to Appendices
Rr ROQUIER	Sept 26		Section Routine	
"	27		Section Routine	
"	28		5 horses + 1 mule evacuated to No. 22 Veterinary Hospital. Owing to close proximity to ABBEVILLE animals were walked in to hospital. 2 horses admitted sick. admitted 3 horses and 1 mule sick	
"	29		Ambulance proceeded to ANGENVILLERS to collect from lists of 10 LANCS FUSILIERS animals left by 1st INDIAN CAVALRY DIVISION when on line of March. 3 animals admitted sick.	
"	30		When Section moved to CRINCOURT animals were evacuated from MONDICOURT Station by Convoys of FRENCH and of ENGLISH Railway Wagons. Owing two convoys no difficulty was experienced as it takes only 30 minutes from section to station to which the sick from Safety Rail Head no 14 kms was.	

J Steward Capt.
OC 29 MVS

CONFIDENTIAL

Vol 16

WAR DIARY

29 Mobile Vet Section

October 1916

Army Form C. 2118.

WAR DIARY
or
INTELLIGENCE SUMMARY

29. Mobile Veterinary Section
October 1916.
page I.

(Erase heading not required.)

Instructions regarding War Diaries and Intelligence Summaries are contained in F. S. Regs, Part II. and the Staff Manual respectively. Title Pages will be prepared in manuscript.

Place	Date	Hour	Summary of Events and Information	Remarks and references to Appendices
ACHEUX	1		Section Routine. Section attended Church parade with Divisional H.Q.	
"	2		1 N.C.O. and 3 men proceeded to Le PONCHELLE and VILLEROY to collect 4 animals that had been inspected by O.C. The sick transport proceeded with 11 horses to NO. 22 VETERINARY HOSPITAL Took 10 horses and 1 mule.	
"	3		3 animals admitted to sick lines. 2 animals admitted sick. Ambulance float proceeded to VILLEROY to collect sick animal left by A/79 Artillery.	
"	4		1 horse admitted to sick lines. Ambulance proceeded to La PONCHAL to convey sick animal left by A/81 Artillery.	
"	5		O.C. proceeded to AUXI-LE-CHATEAU to inspect animals left by 78 Bde Artillery and to ascertain that 16.75 animals who the minimum allowance and not 26 or 50 centime as this man had made out for himself.	
"	6		Ambulance proceeded to NEUVILLE-LE-HOPITAL to collect animal reported both DORSET's but animal had improved and Ambulance was not required. Yesterday was a long and	

2449 Wt. W14957/Mgo 750,000 1/16 J.B.C. & A. Forms/C.2118/12.

Army Form C. 2118.

WAR DIARY
or
INTELLIGENCE SUMMARY

29. Mobile Veterinary Station
October 1916. page 2.

(Erase heading not required.)

Place	Date	Hour	Summary of Events and Information	Remarks and references to Appendices
St RIQUIER	5		1 N.C.O and 3 men proceeded to 22 VETERINARY HOSPITAL with 2 sick horses. Ambulance conveyed 5 sick & 2 wounded. Animals came into section. O.C. visited on afternoon and as the section was marching back to the front next day the O.C. asked for both Ambulance and obtaining Same got the animals away.	
St RIQUIER CONTEVILLE	6		Section marched at 11.30 a.m and arrived at 12 noon at 50 Infantry Bde group to CONTEVILLE & distance 7/10 kilometres	
CONTEVILLE MEZEROLLE	7		Section marched at 10 a.m and continued march to MEZEROLLE arriving 3 p.m. & knott a man was detailed to collect animals that O.C. inspected at AUXI-LE-CHATEAU. Man arrived with animals in evening to take description of it. Collected	
MEZEROLLE	8		"Standing to" on examination of animal being horse it was found that it was not an English horse but a French Arabian and to Ulphleate enquiries O.C. with one man rode back to AUXI-LE-CHATEAU to get proper horse which we done & front arrival left. The man (a knutte) said that owing to the state of his animal	

Army Form C. 2118.

WAR DIARY
or
INTELLIGENCE SUMMARY

29 Mobile Veterinary Section
October 1916. page 2

(Erase heading not required.)

Place	Date	Hour	Summary of Events and Information	Remarks and references to Appendices
MEZEROLLE	8		A horse kept for transport purposes was given up. 1 horse evacuated from BARLY.	
MEZEROLLE & PAS.	9		Section paraded at 8.45 a.m. and horse chest independently to PAS. & to DOULLENS. arriving at PAS. 1.30 p.m. when section became a Field run PAS. Yards have fortunately taken over for our stores. The horse chest from DI RICOUIER & PAS has also owing to their having hutts & sanitary groups the trenches no one to have and huts. We who have lived as at the horse had without any untoward incident to note.	
PAS. GRINCOURT	10		4 animals admitted sick. owing to change of area the section was fortunate to obtain billets formerly held at GRINCOURT. and these stables etc had been built for winter quarters.	
GRINCOURT	11		Section horse chest away to GRINCOURT a 15 mm Go horse.	
"	12		4 animals admitted sick. The section entrained 135 horses to the 2nd Kitchener numerous sick animal. This was quite a good effort seeing that the Section from Advanced Horse hospital Ambulance proceeded to FITZROY & Advs Sick Animal.	

2449 Wt. W14957/Mg0 750,000 1/16 J.B.C. & A. Forms/C.2118/12.

Army Form C. 2118.

WAR DIARY
or
INTELLIGENCE SUMMARY   29 Mobile Veterinary Section
(Erase heading not required.)   October 1916.   page 4

Instructions regarding War Diaries and Intelligence Summaries are contained in F. S. Regs., Part II. and the Staff Manual respectively. Title Pages will be prepared in manuscript.

Place	Date	Hour	Summary of Events and Information	Remarks and references to Appendices
RINCOURT	12		O.C. 1 N.C.O and 4 men proceed to MONDICOURT to evacuate 7 horses and 1 mule to NO 23. VETERINARY HOSPITAL.	
"	13		O.C. 1 N.C.O and 4 men proceeded to MONDICOURT & evacuated 7 horses to NO.23 VETERINARY HOSPITAL. Ambulance proceeded to BAYENCOURT to collect a sick animal.	
"	14		Ambulance collected sick horse from TOWN MAJOR of MONDICOURT. This was a French civilian horse and was injured in an act of accident by English motor lorry. Animal sustained serious injury to coronary band but however it was on old animal so charger as almost cured when section CR in court arr on 19-10-16. Ambulance also collected from 7 LINCOLNS 1 mule, 3 horses and 2 horses admitted to sick lines.	
"	15		Section Routine	
"	16		23 animals admitted sick - all cases fat deliveries from divisional Artillery	

Army Form C. 2118.

WAR DIARY
or
INTELLIGENCE SUMMARY
29 Mobile Veterinary Section

October 1916. page 2.

(Erase heading not required.)

Place	Date	Hour	Summary of Events and Information	Remarks and references to Appendices
BRINCOURT	17		Collected animals left by 33 DIVISIONAL SIGNAL CO. at HENU. O.C. 2 N.C.O.S and 10 men proceeded to MONDICOURT to evacuate 23 horses and 1 mule to 22 VETERINARY HOSPITAL. 31 horses and 3 mules admitted sick – all cases of DEBILITY from DIVISIONAL ARTILLERY. The large number of cases of Debility was due to the guns and animals had just to be carrying up Ammunition to firing line. Ambulance collected sick horse left at SOUASTRE by 19 BRIGADE (INFANTRY) 33. DIVISION.	
"	18		N.C.O who was in Charge of evacuation party reported he was 43 hours in the truck with his horses. Ambulance collected from 27 RESERVE PARK. A.S.C Sick horse. 4 horses admitted to sick lines.	
"	19		O.C. 2 N.C.O.S + 12 men proceeded to SAULTY to evacuate 33 animals to 22 VETERINARY HOSPITAL. Ambulance breaking his journeys to convey animals. 1 horse admitted dies	

WAR DIARY
or
INTELLIGENCE SUMMARY

Army Form C. 2118

29th Mobile Veterinary Section
October 1916 page 6

(Erase heading not required.)

Place	Date	Hour	Summary of Events and Information	Remarks and references to Appendices
CRICOURT	20		Ambulance collected sick horse from 77 Co. R.E. at SUS ASTRE. 18 horses evacuated to 22 VETERINARY HOSPITAL. 3 new admission sick. Received one.	
"	21		Ambulance collected from 148 Co. A.S.C. at DOULLENS one sick horse. Marked sick.	
"	22		Section moved at 8 am (personnel on line) to TREUX at 10 am arriving at 6-30 pm Route was via PAS. AUTHIE. VAUCHELLES. LOUDENCOURT. LUCHEUX. SOUASTRE. HENENCOURT. LAVIEVILLE to BUIRE and TREUX. We ran up fighting line was taken and horses had continually to be put by columns of lorries horse things. We had no ambulances and no casualties ammunition & remounts to not	
TREUX	23		Section Romaine. "Standing to" in district. Standing to" D.A.V.S. 4th Army. Col. Hunt inspected section & inspected entire section with the town and admitted sick horse	DSC

WAR DIARY
or
INTELLIGENCE SUMMARY

Army Form C. 2118

29 Mobile Veterinary Section

October 1916. page 7.

Place	Date	Hour	Summary of Events and Information	Remarks and references to Appendices
TREUX	25.		Ambulance collected from 147 Coy ASC at CARCAILLOT farm. 1 sick horse. "Standing to"	
"	26		Evacuated 7 horses to No. 7 VETERINARY HOSPITAL TOWN M[ile]P[ost] to R. MERICOURT, handed over sick horse left by 1/2 Co. R.E. 3 sick horses and 1 mule admitted.	
TREUX to MEAULTE	27		Section paraded at 9 am and car chef to MEAULTE at 10 am with Division. A long time no tea on the way as the ambulance going to the great congestion of traffic and various units having two churns at intervals of two kilo.	
MEAULTE	28		Standing to. Ambulance collected from IV Corps HS. 1 sick horse.	
"	29		Standing to. 9 horses admitted sick.	
"	30		Standing to. O.C. IN O.O. and S. new pressence E.CROSS TOWN Co evacuate 11 horses + 1 mule to NO. 7 VETERINARY HOSPITAL. 5 horses admitted sick.	
MEAULTE MINDEN POST.	31		Section paraded at 8 am and her chef to MINDEN POST. Owing to the congested state	

WAR DIARY
or
INTELLIGENCE SUMMARY

Army Form C. 2118

39. Mobile Veterinary Section

October 1916 page 8

Place	Date	Hour	Summary of Events and Information	Remarks and references to Appendices
MEAULTE MINDEN POST			I took 4 horses has taken to x00 a distance of 1 Kilometre. O.C decided to try the use of trucks across country and though these were very unwilling and performed a function and destroy. Survey was performed as usual. In going over the ground to position as usual. The ground at times was slow & laborious. It arrived at position it was found that the MOBILE SECTION of 8th Division had not moved out two causes of inconvenience. This section "obstructed up" for the night and decided to make a new position & try a number & tourney was done. The Cart was kept moving and tonight evacuation of sick animals though wasn't able for the reception of sick & had a distance of 200 yards very convenient.	

J.J.Kunkel Capt. O.C. 39 M.V.S.

Army Form C. 2118.

29 Mobile Veterinary Section
November 1916

WAR DIARY
or
INTELLIGENCE SUMMARY
(Erase heading not required.)

Place	Date	Hour	Summary of Events and Information	Remarks and references to Appendices
MINDEN POST.	1.		Camp moved nearer to road owing to long muddy approach to horse lines. Space taken over being too cramped & confined.	
"	2.		Effort was made to get into CARNOY but becomes so that the personnel might have the benefit of the drys, onto there there have shelters from the weather but night but CARNOY was not available owing to the number of troops about there. 4 horses to horses admitted sick.	
"	3.		A site near MANSELL COPSE has been selected after a great difficulty for M.V.S. tents and shelters for the men being procured from MANSELL CAMP. Hospital from PLATEAU Siding. 9 horses and 2 mules have been evacuated to No. 7 Veterinary M.V.S. camp & rail head having shelled but without doing any damage to the section so it had moved out to vicinity above the road PRICOURT-MARICOURT	

Army Form C. 2118.

WAR DIARY
or
INTELLIGENCE SUMMARY.

29 Mobile Veterinary Section

November 1916

(Erase heading not required.)

Instructions regarding War Diaries and Intelligence Summaries are contained in F. S. Regs., Part II. and the Staff Manual respectively. Title pages will be prepared in manuscript.

Place	Date	Hour	Summary of Events and Information	Remarks and references to Appendices
MANSELL-COPSE	4		Erecting new sick lines and shelters for men and stores on a comparatively clean area though adjacent to camp for a short distance was very bad.	
"	5		31 horses evacuated to No.7 Veterinary Hospital from PLATEAU. owing to Knitted hair shed when tucking the animals.	
"	6		42 Animals admitted to Section. 23 Animals evacuated to No.7 Veterinary Hospital 22 Animals admitted to Section	
"	7		47 Animals evacuated to No.7 Veterinary Hospital. 3 Animals (horses) destroyed in Section from debility. Animals being in a most emaciated condition and unable to rise 1/6 the ground where they lay. 9 Animals admitted sick	
"	8		23 Animals evacuated to No.7 Veterinary Hospital 1 Destitute Case died. 1 " " Shot.	

Army Form C. 2118.

WAR DIARY
or
INTELLIGENCE SUMMARY.

29 Mobile Veterinary Section

November 1916

(Erase heading not required.)

Instructions regarding War Diaries and Intelligence Summaries are contained in F. S. Regs., Part II. and the Staff Manual respectively. Title pages will be prepared in manuscript.

Place	Date	Hour	Summary of Events and Information	Remarks and references to Appendices
MANSELL COPSE	8		39 Animals admitted sick	
"	9		32 Animals evacuated to No.7. Veterinary Hospital from PLATEAU. Sixty admitted sick 44 horses.	
"	10		30 animals evacuated to No.7. Veterinary Hospital 1 mule shot. 7 horses admitted sick	
"	11		11 Animals evacuated to No.7. Veterinary Hospital 3 cases being mange & these 3 cases meant one attendant from my depleted staff being over 5 & so many new being down at the base with sick horses. 2 horses shot (in) debility 9 horses admitted sick	
"	12		8 animals evacuated to No.7. Veterinary Hospital 9 Animals admitted sick	

JMc

Army Form C. 2118.

WAR DIARY
or
INTELLIGENCE SUMMARY.

(Erase heading not required.)

39 Mobile Veterinary Section

November 1916

Place	Date	Hour	Summary of Events and Information	Remarks and references to Appendices
MANSELL COPSE	13		40 animals evacuated to No. 7 Veterinary Hospital admitted sick 30 horses.	
"	14		The 40 animals to be evacuated on 13th has been kept back owing to shortage of trucks - these were now evacuated and from PLATEAU Siding - Rail been being shelled at the time.	
			32 animals admitted sick.	
"	15		54 animals evacuated to No. 7 Veterinary Hospital. Section marched with Numeros to Rest Area at CAVILLON. March was made at 9am and the road was very bad as far as BECORDEL the traffic being also very congested. Section has marched with only 13 men owing to the large frequent evacuations men were away at the base and 6 men into home down the line here so dead to report on arrival back at PLATEAU to O.C. No.46 M.V.S. & seems that unit to its evacuation though no assistance has been to my section.	

A5834. Wt.W4973/M687. 750,000 8/16 D.D.&L.Ltd. Forms/C.2118/13.

WAR DIARY or INTELLIGENCE SUMMARY

Army Form C. 2118.

29 Mobile Veterinary Section

November 1916

Place	Date	Hour	Summary of Events and Information	Remarks and references to Appendices
INSELL COPSE	5		and orders to proceed to our position the MARICOURT — MARICOURT Road were received. The position of the M.V.S. in itself was not over satisfactory owing to the congestion of Camps & the bad state of the Route Veterinaire was limited, believing though there was so far away & a tench was hooked up to the hut from it went & the sick horses. The care & attention necessary for the Riding horses & personnel of M.V.S was for owing to lack of men to exercise them. This had owing to lack of men to exercise them. This knees were only littered once a day & then the batmans time was 2 miles off. The other service these animals had was going to water – grooming thus was none. On one occasion only the senior Sergeant, O.C & 1 batman was all that was left to the M.V.S/ to look after the sicker animals & 90 sick as well for watering, feeding etc as well as hooking and assembling returns	

Army Form C. 2118.

WAR DIARY
or
INTELLIGENCE SUMMARY.
(Erase heading not required.)

29/Mobile Veterinary Section
November 1916

Place	Date	Hour	Summary of Events and Information	Remarks and references to Appendices
MANSELL COPSE	15		Cover the Base hospitals has supplied to men for the 3 M.V.S's in this area most could have been carried on as smoothly as on the July 1st Operations as if the M.V.S was back out of the congested area such as MEAULTE when the fighting through. Thus had out an advanced post at CARNOY it would have killed greatly as a few men carried there from there there animals + M.V.S moved have several Railheads to send animals to at GROVETOWN, EDGE HILL & ALBERT. PLATEAU. riding bus but a small withers it was to open a scramble to get emfrrans knives to clean the ties. Section halted fed at MERICOURT marching through CORBIE huts at DAOURS for the night The breather was very cold last thing men cold was made a good time without casualties.	

Army Form C. 2118.

WAR DIARY
or
INTELLIGENCE SUMMARY

Army Veterinary Section

November 1916

(Erase heading not required.)

Place	Date	Hour	Summary of Events and Information	Remarks and references to Appendices
AMIENS to OISSY	16	9am	Hors Ch. who continued through to AMIENS to OISSY where section had ch. Billets for men & ch. a dugo for horses though to the open ground. The day was again very cold but the day march was made in excellent time throughout incidents.	
OISSY	17		Making conditions for men & horses as comportable as possible owing to all being dirtied. Horses exercised, kits & used ch. had to see about equipping section & men with him to complete. Took over ch's & wagons t charge of 50 Inf. M. Bde. 147 Co. A.S.C. 50 men from Inf. Co. 53 Fried animals and 17 Signal Co.	
"	18		Section routine & ch.s incidence Hd.a + 50 Inf. Bde groom.	
"	19		admitted sick 3. ch's: duties Equipment Section	

Army Form C. 2118.

WAR DIARY
or
INTELLIGENCE SUMMARY.

No 3 Mobile Veterinary Section

November 1916

(Erase heading not required.)

Instructions regarding War Diaries and Intelligence Summaries are contained in F.S. Regs., Part II. and the Staff Manual respectively. Title pages will be prepared in manuscript.

Place	Date	Hour	Summary of Events and Information	Remarks and references to Appendices
OISSY	20		A.D.V.S. Antries. Inspected 50 Supply Bn. Group. This Group was very scattered over a large tract to rest area. 1 horse admitted sick	
"	21		8 animals admitted sick at a.D.V.S. 3rd Army Group.	
"	22		40 animals evacuated for GUARD'S ARTILLERY from HANGEST to No.7 VETERINARY. Owing to the fact of this Artillery coming out of the line the large numbers of animals for evacuation necessitated the whole G.D.V.S. 4th Army to have the animals left at the front until GUARDS M.V.S. returned – This was done on 27th a.D.V.S. 4th Army.	
"	23		4 animals admitted sick & inspected 50 Supply Bn. Group. – & No 7 a.D.V.S.	
"	24		8 animals evacuated to No 7 Veterinary Hospital from HANGEST on 4th a.D.V.S.	

WAR DIARY or INTELLIGENCE SUMMARY

Army Form C. 2118.

29 Mobile Veterinary Section November 1916

Place	Date	Hour	Summary of Events and Information	Remarks and references to Appendices
OISSY	25		29 Animals evacuated from GUARDS ARTILLERY at HANGEST to No.7 Veterinary Hospital as there if and S. hospital H.B. Group.	
"	26		Horses so lost by B de Group. otherwise f and S. Animals admitted sick.	
"	27		2 mules unable to walk were taken to 22 VETERINARY HOSPITAL by motor ambulance as there if and S. Reputed sickness, horse kits equipment at there if and S.	
"	28		60 animals of GUARDS. ARTILLERY evacuated from HANGEST to No.7 Veterinary Hospital	
"	29		1 cow (mare) received from GUARDS ARTILLERY	

Army Form C. 2118.

WAR DIARY
or INTELLIGENCE SUMMARY.

Squad Mobile Veterinary Section

No. 10

November 1916.

(Erase heading not required.)

Instructions regarding War Diaries and Intelligence Summaries are contained in F. S. Regs., Part II. and the Staff Manual respectively. Title pages will be prepared in manuscript.

Place	Date	Hour	Summary of Events and Information	Remarks and references to Appendices
OISSY	30		at this M.V.S. Inspected 50 Arty Bde Group. 8 animals evacuated from MANCEST to No 7 Veterinary Hospital	

J.P. Kennel Capt. S.
O.C. 29 M.V.S.

1/11/16

Army Form C. 2118.

WAR DIARY
or
INTELLIGENCE SUMMARY
(Erase heading not required.)

29 Mobile Veterinary Section

December 1916

Vol / 8

Place	Date	Hour	Summary of Events and Information	Remarks and references to Appendices
ISSY	1		22 Animals admitted sick	
"	2		23 animals evacuated to N.O.7 Veterinary Hospital from HANGEST. Ambulance conveying one case. Ambulance collected arrival of GUARDS ARTILLERY from LE QUESNOY. Mobile Ambulance came from NO.22 Veterinary Hospital ABBEVILLE to collect his very lame horses. 8 horses admitted sick.	
"	3		11 Animals evacuated to NO.22 Veterinary Hospital from HANGEST. Ambulance one case. Ambulance brought to station the night before one other case a man being left with it. 17 Animals admitted sick.	
"	4		Ambulance proceeded to LE MESGE to collect sick animals. 29 Animals evacuated from HANGEST to NO.7 Veterinary Hospital. 16 Animals admitted sick	

Army Form C. 2118.

WAR DIARY
or
INTELLIGENCE SUMMARY.

29 Mobile Veterinary Section
December 1916

(Erase heading not required.)

Instructions regarding War Diaries and Intelligence Summaries are contained in F. S. Regs., Part II. and the Staff Manual respectively. Title pages will be prepared in manuscript.

Place	Date	Hour	Summary of Events and Information	Remarks and references to Appendices
	5.		1 mule admitted sick.	
	6.		Season Routine	
	7-31.		O.C. on sick leave	

J.J. Runnels
Cork
O.C. 29 M.V.S.

A.5834. Wt.W4973/M687. 750,000. 8/16. D. D. & L. Ltd. Forms/C.2118/13.

Army Form C. 2118.

WAR DIARY
or
INTELLIGENCE SUMMARY.

(Erase heading not required.)

January 1917   29 mules very sick

Vol 19

Instructions regarding War Diaries and Intelligence Summaries are contained in F. S. Regs., Part II. and the Staff Manual respectively. Title pages will be prepared in manuscript.

Place	Date	Hour	Summary of Events and Information	Remarks and references to Appendices
MINDEN-POST	1-6		O.C. on Sick Leave.	
"	7		24 Animals admitted to sick lines.	
"	8		Ambulance proceded to "HAPPY VALLEY" to collect sick animals. 33 animals evacuated from PLATEAU station to No. 7 Veterinary Hospital. 63 animals admitted sick.	
"	9		32 Animals evacuated from PLATEAU Station to No. 7 Veterinary hospital. 1 mule destroyed. 20 animals evacuated in afternoon from PLATEAU to No. 7 Veterinary Hospital. 38 admitted sick.	
"	10		36 animals evacuated from PLATEAU to No. 7 Veterinary Hospital. 51 Animals admitted sick.	
"	11		81 animals evacuated from PLATEAU for No.7 Veterinary hospital. 1 horse destroyed. 26 animals admitted sick.	

Army Form C. 2118.

WAR DIARY
or
INTELLIGENCE SUMMARY.
(Erase heading not required.)

January 1917. 2 Mobile Veterinary Section

Instructions regarding War Diaries and Intelligence Summaries are contained in F. S. Regs., Part II. and the Staff Manual respectively. Title pages will be prepared in manuscript.

Place	Date	Hour	Summary of Events and Information	Remarks and references to Appendices
MILLENCOURT POST.	12		15 Animals evacuated from PLATEAU to NO.7. Veterinary hospital. 18 Animals evacuated from PLATEAU in afternoon to NO.7 Veterinary Hospital. 1 horse destroyed. 95 Animals admitted sick.	
"	13		24 Animals admitted sick.	
"	14		29 Animals evacuated from PLATEAU to NO.7. Veterinary hospital. 2 Animals destroyed. Ambulance arrived. Sick mule from MEAULTE. 29 Animals admitted sick.	
"	15		27 Animals evacuated from PLATEAU to NO.7. Veterinary hospital. Advance party sent to take over Billets at CORBIE & Divisional Rest area.	
"	16		Section turned at 5am for march to Amarmond Rest area at CORBIE. The march was much in very good time to order. No incidents occurred en Route. Arrived CORBIE. Section billeted at MERICOURT to later. Arrived CORBIE 1.0C Rm.	

Army Form C. 2118.

WAR DIARY
or
INTELLIGENCE SUMMARY.
(Erase heading not required.)

3   January 1917   29th Mobile Veterinary Section

Place	Date	Hour	Summary of Events and Information	Remarks and references to Appendices
MEZEN- PONT- CORBIE	16		Section Billeted near BRAY-ROAD. Accommodation for the horses being gone over for the few men to carry from. 4 Animals left by 18th I.V.S. 29. Diseases were taken over. 7 Animals admitted Sick.	
CORBIE	17		6 animals evacuated from CORBIE to No. 7 Veterinary Hospital. Dung Sheet to ground 9. cleaning of section lines men busy. 8 Animals admitted sick.	
"	18		7 animals evacuated from CORBIE to No. 7 Veterinary Hospital. 2 animals cast by D.D.V.S. 4th Army for service admitted to section. 3 animals admitted sick.	
"	19		O.C. visited VAUX-SUR-SOMME to arrange inspect of animals & to arrange for their collection by M.V.S.	

WAR DIARY or INTELLIGENCE SUMMARY

Army Form C. 2118.

January 1917. 29 Mobile Veterinary Section

Place	Date	Hour	Summary of Events and Information	Remarks and references to Appendices
CORBIE	20		1 N.C.O and 2 men proceeded to VAUX-SUR-SOMME to cast 3 animals. 6 animals admitted. Cast for hire by D.D.V.S. 4th Army. 13 animals admitted died.	
"	21		19 Animals evacuated from CORBIE to No.7 Veterinary hospital. 2 animals destroyed in shelter - Animals were evacuated at own shelter - As had been sent into M.V.S. 4 animals admitted sick.	
"	22		Ambulance took 3 Animals to F. 195 Army Battery. R.G.A. & dealt 3 sick Animals.	
"	23		13 Animals evacuated from CORBIE to No.7. Veterinary hospital. 2 animals admitted sick.	
"	24		2 animals destroyed. 3 animals admitted sick.	
"	25		2 animals admitted sick.	

Army Form C. 2118.

WAR DIARY
or
INTELLIGENCE SUMMARY.
(Erase heading not required.)

29 Mobile Veterinary Section

January 1917

Instructions regarding War Diaries and Intelligence Summaries are contained in F. S. Regs., Part II. and the Staff Manual respectively. Title pages will be prepared in manuscript.

Place	Date	Hour	Summary of Events and Information	Remarks and references to Appendices
CORBIE	26.		Got Section things together over advance party to the front sent on advance party.	
"	27		Section transport paraded with led horses at 7am and then and to MINDEN POST under Senior N.C.O. O.C. with 2 N.C.O's and 8 men stayed behind to entrain 11 animals from CORBIE at 11am. Y.O.C. with men then proceeded up Guest track to MINDEN POST and took over from the M.V.S. of the 20th Division.	
"	28		7 Sick animals admitted. saving sloven section lines etc.	
"	29		Section Routine 1 Animal admitted Sick	
"	30		1 animal admitted sick	
"	31		1 animal transferred to the prolonged post to divnl supply of late owing to the prolonged post to divnl supply of late was greatly felt by the Section especially the watering of sick animals.	

J P Kennel Capt
OC 29 M.V.S.

31/1

Army Form C. 2118.

WAR DIARY
or
INTELLIGENCE SUMMARY.

29 Mobile Veterinary Section
February 1917.

Vol 2 O

Place	Date	Hour	Summary of Events and Information	Remarks and references to Appendices
MINDEN POST.	1.		One animal admitted sick. One animal destroyed.	
"	2.		One animal admitted sick.	
"	3.		3 animals admitted sick - stray animals	
"	4.		Section Routine	
"	5.		Section Routine - Improving on and adding new huts to existing accommodation. Material supplied by R.E.	
"	6.		Animal are cell and sick horse pen at Echo huts hospital. One animal admitted sick.	
"	7.		Section Routine.	
"	8.		3 animals admitted sick.	
"	9.		One stray animal admitted sick. One animal destroyed.	

WAR DIARY or INTELLIGENCE SUMMARY

Army Form C. 2118.

29 Mob'l'e Vety Section

February 1917

Place	Date	Hour	Summary of Events and Information	Remarks and references to Appendices
MINDEN - POST.	10		Section Routine - Improving accommodation for sick.	
"	11		1 animal admitted sick. 1 stray animal admitted sick.	
"	12		1 mule shot. 11 animals admitted sick	
"	13		1 animal shot. 27 animals evacuated from PLATEAU to NO. 7. VETERINARY. HOSPITAL. Owing to the traffic restrictions no trucks were available for the use of sick animals. Units were advised of this & consequently few animals were sent to this section. What few that were taken in were bad cases also the stray animals who had to be put through mullein bath.	
"	14		4 animals admitted sick. 1 stray animal received sick.	
"	15		19 animals admitted sick. Ambulance made two journeys to the D.A.C. to collect sick animals.	

WAR DIARY
or
INTELLIGENCE SUMMARY.

Army Form C. 2118.

29 Mobile Vety Section
February 1917.

Place	Date	Hour	Summary of Events and Information	Remarks and references to Appendices
MINSEN-POST	16.		1 animal admitted Sick	
	17.		1 animal admitted sick 1 animal destroyed	
"	18		22 Animals admitted sick	
"	19		Ambulance convoy sick horse from 93. CVRE. One animal destroyed. 4 animals discharged cured. 3 animals admitted sick.	
"	20		46 animals evacuated from PLATEAU & NO. 7. VETERINARY. HOSPITAL. FORGES-LES-EAUX. Ambulance conveying his cases to Richebois.	
"–HEILLY	21	9.30 A.M.	Section moved to new area with Divisions + had H.Q at HEILLY where good accommodation was found for the horses and stores. That of the men being from the horse standpoint made in good time further moves and arrival being first a shortage. During the tour of duty	

WAR DIARY
INTELLIGENCE SUMMARY

Army Form C. 2118.

39 Mobile Vety Section

February 1917

Place	Date	Hour	Summary of Events and Information	Remarks and references to Appendices
El Lg.			As the front the Section was not had to inspect unit owing to the restrictions in traffic. Sick animals were treated in unit sick lines - further some of the units of the division had contagious lymphangitis this prevented units from using the public service for fear of them being a flying disease to the Base. A severe frost is due to the whole time of the restrictions in traffic. The being carried at a minimum & this sick as the majority of this case treated at the lines. Owing to the severity of the weather and Mud & the general rushed the heart patients in general - several of our men have had to be evacuated to Cavalry Clearing Stations.	
	29		Amb't ammt collected sick horse from D.T. HOURS. 3 animals received from D.D.R. 4th Army. 2 animals admitted Sick.	

Army Form C. 2118.

WAR DIARY
or
INTELLIGENCE SUMMARY.

29 Mobile Vety Section
February 1917

(Erase heading not required.)

Place	Date	Hour	Summary of Events and Information	Remarks and references to Appendices
MEILLY	23		5 animals admitted sick.	
"	24		3 animals admitted sick	
"	25		2 animals admitted sick	
"	26		8 animals admitted sick	
"	27		25 animals evacuated from MERICOURT to NO. 2. VETERINARY HOSPITAL	
			2 animals admitted sick.	
			one animal shot.	
"	28		3 animals discharged cured.	
			1 animal shot.	
			Owing not to horse lines ophthalmic we take thing for the section to Ergnikheaux owing to convenience at the front the wastage however carefully guarded was great.	

P.B. Nunnel Capt.
O.C. 29 Mob. Vet. Sec.
1-3-17.

Army Form C. 2118.

WAR DIARY
or
INTELLIGENCE SUMMARY.

(Erase heading not required.)

29. MOBILE VETERINARY SECTION.

March 1917.

Vol 2

Place	Date	Hour	Summary of Events and Information	Remarks and references to Appendices

During the month of March the Section was one of the busiest it has ever had owing to numbers of animals being evacuated and Debarkers were received and evacuated were compared to previous cases that required washing out from the Unit. The Drilling Type Examined by other Units who in certain Examinations also noticed Cow hair.

94 animals were received during March 10 were sent to Remounts and 2 that were only fair specimens. These were sent by road from ABBEVILLE to a Veterinary Hospital. The System of sending animals by road never seemed to be a success as remounts not confined to riding but also for Lorry teams and cart wheels and of accident at 15' Convoys Sections to Watering places of Remounts were admitted for inspection, and of these 4 were admitted sick. The remainder being mixed Drivers and cart drivers.

59 animals were evacuated of which 33 were of the Mange or "animals suspected to others being from cases they being examined. Being mainly Debility cases, and were being examined and inspected ofd. 93 C/RE, 7 cases of Mange prevailed.

MOVES. During the month the Section was billeted at HEILLY.

A5834 Wt. W4973/M687 750,000 8/16 D.D. & L. Ltd. Forms/C.2118/13.

WAR DIARY or INTELLIGENCE SUMMARY

Army Form C. 2118.

29 MOBILE VETERINARY SECTION

March 1917

HARPONVILLE, WILLEMAN and LE CAUROY.

HARPONVILLE: With the exception of Harponville good cover and standing were found for the horses and the hard frost could make one of the mud a source no are to hid the sick animals efficiently. At Harponville the horse lines were on a hard patch and shelter was erected close to where sick and injured animals.

MARCHES: During the march from Harponville to Willeman the section had a van of 50th Infantry Bde Group taking 3 days. The march was very slow and frequent halts were made at all times and the halting on hills was noticeable. I had been tried to let the Section have one day and have been definitely not clear up the Sick horses left on the line of March by the Units - The Section had supplies for 4 days so that there was no need to draw at Supply Dumps en Route. The Section marched daily from Willeman to Brigade Group.

LE CAUROY and at this base ratio factory, horses passed in good time

WAR DIARY
INTELLIGENCE SUMMARY

Army Form C. 2118.

29 MOBILE VETERINARY SECTION.

March 1917

Place	Date	Hour	Summary of Events and Information	Remarks and references to Appendices

so that horses could be quickly erected and the section prepared for the [next] reception of sick.

During some days to the back area a number of advancing horses left on the line of march had to be and it have ambulance was sent to truck me.

At WILLEMAN advanced mobile of proximity to ABBEVILLE to track the sick horses to hospital in a day. The horse ambulance conveying the time animals to evacuate were made & going by road may have relieved congestion of Railway traffic.

J. Skinner
Capt.
O.C. 29 Mob Vet Sect

Army Form C. 2118.

29 Mobile Vety Section

WAR DIARY
or
INTELLIGENCE SUMMARY.
(Erase heading not required.)

April 1917   Vol 2

Place	Date	Hour	Summary of Events and Information	Remarks and references to Appendices
LE CAUROY	1-8 April		The Section at LE CAUROY at Divisional rest area. The bulk of the Section began dig the erection of animals left on the line of March by units was heavy and after long chick ances was covered. The Animals Casualties were in a very bad state of debility and several had to be shot while a few had been already shot disposed of before the Section collected them. The horse Ambulance had to make frequent journeys conveying sick and injured animals to either rail-head or Section. During this period only a small number of cases were admitted for treatment and evacuations were light. Advantage was taken of the rest to equit the Section harness + horse rt appliances in technical equipment	

A5834 Wt. W4973/M687 750,000 8/16 D. D. & L. Ltd. Forms/C.2118/13.

Army Form C. 2118.

WAR DIARY
or
INTELLIGENCE SUMMARY.

(Erase heading not required.)

Army Form C. 2118.

29. Hostile Vimy Sector
April 1917

Instructions regarding War Diaries and Intelligence Summaries are contained in F. S. Regs., Part II. and the Staff Manual respectively. Title pages will be prepared in manuscript.

Place	Date	Hour	Summary of Events and Information	Remarks and references to Appendices
LE CAUROY	1-8 April		He visits the Section accepted here very good. Excellent standings with cover for the horses that enabled one to avoid horse lines and kits being as aseptic as to the ambulance animals were drawn from extreme. The weather during our stay at LE CAUROY was very bad but with frequent snowstorms & much rain. PREVENT a diet one of throttles away who kept as rail head for Avrance to No 22 Veterinary hospital.	
BERNEVILLE	8-12 April		Section moved forward with C echelon of HQ Division to BERNEVILLE and stood to. A first aid was started for the section with standings near for the horses. At BERNEVILLE the Section was prepared to move forward through ARRAS when the Division advanced. A number of horses and	

A5834 Wt.W4973/M687 750,000 8/16 D.D.&L.Ltd. Forms/C.2118/13.

Army Form C. 2118.

WAR DIARY
or
INTELLIGENCE SUMMARY.
(Erase heading not required.)

29 Mobile Vety Section
April 1917

Place	Date	Hour	Summary of Events and Information	Remarks and references to Appendices
BERNEVILLE	8-IV.		Cavalry horses on their previous "here" dumped on "the Section" so these animals had to be evacuated it reduced our personnel a interfered with our mobility to so through the advance. the Cavalry Mobile Sections should have brought their injured animals to the M.V.S at rest had who have supplied with extra men from the Base for this purpose. At BERNEVILLE the heaths was very het and roads very bad that of large two-wheeled mo very het and roads for injured animals delivery fast cars to travel over. AC NEZ-LES-DUSIANS, Stretchers away was not kept for No. 29 Veterinary Hospital.	
ARRAS.	17-13.		The Section moved found billeted him the BLANG? road	

WAR DIARY or INTELLIGENCE SUMMARY

Army Form C. 2118.

29 Mobile Vety Section
April 1917

Place	Date	Hour	Summary of Events and Information	Remarks and references to Appendices
ARRAS	2-13		A Gronol factory being used for horse lines a french horse attaining for the men. The Section was standing by and prepared to advance further. The section billets was a good one though exposed to shell fire. Owing to the alteration in the tactical situation the Section was ordered to leave ARRAS for AGNEZ-LES-DUISANS the supply was short.	
AGNEZ-LES-DUISANS	13-25		A good position was secured at AGNEZ with a lot of covered space for sick horses. This site we had been led on which was a great benefit and we had no lot up we yards away, having huts at the Stables was a great saving of time especially when one had to hundre dress to water as animals coming from the front greatly weakened a lot of good water.	

Army Form C. 2118.

WAR DIARY
or
INTELLIGENCE SUMMARY.

(Erase heading not required.)

29 Mobile Vety Section

April 1917

Instructions regarding War Diaries and Intelligence Summaries are contained in F. S. Regs., Part II. and the Staff Manual respectively. Title pages will be prepared in manuscript.

Place	Date	Hour	Summary of Events and Information	Remarks and references to Appendices
AGNEZ-LES-DUISANS	13.2.5.		An advanced post was established at ARRAS was intended to carry from BEANCY. 1 NCO and 5 men were now here. All animals in the forward area were here collected, dressed & the section at AGNEZ eased during. Owing to the advanced position of this post a large number of animals were saved that might have been otherwise left on the road to unused to the injuries. Animals from a large number of units other than their own were received disposed of. Owing to the large number of animals since evac, the Horse Ambulance of the section though doing several journeys by day & night releves of horses could not cope with it's work	

A5834 Wt. W4973/M687. 750,000 8/16 D. D. & L. Ltd. Forms/C.2118/13.

Army Form C. 2118.

WAR DIARY
or
INTELLIGENCE SUMMARY

29th Field Amb[ulance] Section
April 1917

Place	Date	Hour	Summary of Events and Information	Remarks and references to Appendices
ACHEZ-LES-DUISANS	13	9.5	and the Boer hit the Ambulance Officers Orly who was attached to the section at AGNEZ for 3 days + this Ambulance also escorted hot and cleared a large number of wounded knew. The hard driving these horses had was heavy on the personnel who conducted them to the Base were away for days at a time. No assistance at all was given by the M.V.S. at all send into he had the Base details as this M.V.S. had them out escorted. It is necessary that when the Section is at the front during extreme operations that assistance must be given to augment the personnel as the Section horses must not be lost sight of so the time to be retained upon seemed never existed rather	

WAR DIARY
INTELLIGENCE SUMMARY

Army Form C. 2118.

29 Mobile Vety Section

April 1917.

Place	Date	Hour	Summary of Events and Information	Remarks and references to Appendices
AGNEZ-LES-DUISANS	13-25		An attempt is made & other units it times to have Section turn off for purpose to evacuate large number of animals. The have seem to be army such a long time that the [ ] of the Larger Authorities but the trusted up the men kept to send back women & then clear the animals to evacuate numbers and otherwise.	
H.E. Cauroy	26-30		The Section moved home to its billets at LE CAUROY with the Squadron. There was little work to do as few sick were received. The Section personnel was equipped and schemed stores have up. A short rest was given to the men which was greatly wanted. Animals received 246. Died (as [ ] post) 8 Evacuated 213. Shot 4 Re-board 21.	

W. B. [Signature]
Lt. R.A.V.C.

Army Form C. 2118.

WAR DIARY
or
INTELLIGENCE SUMMARY.
(Erase heading not required.)

29 Mobile Vety Section
17 Division

May 1917

WO 23

Place	Date	Hour	Summary of Events and Information	Remarks and references to Appendices
LE CAUROY	1.		Section moved to forward area with Division and halted	
			for the night further orders at HERMAVILLE.	
HERMAVILLE	2.		Section proceeded to LARESSET and established Section	
LARESSET	12.		for usual work but the division did not stay to go further forward.	
			Only a few horses were received for treatment and evacuation	
			while standing by at LARESSET. 16 horses being received	
			for evacuation - all debility cases.	
LARESSET /			The section moved forward to ARRAS in relief of MVS	
ST NICHOLAS			9th Division and a site was taken in ST NICHOLAS.	
			Whole new ground & in charge for the horses and officers	
			instructed for the procedure to be pursued to supervise dug-outs	

Army Form C. 2118.

WAR DIARY
or
INTELLIGENCE SUMMARY.

(Erase heading not required.)

29 Notes very heavy 17 Divisionan May 1917

Instructions regarding War Diaries and Intelligence Summaries are contained in F. S. Regs., Part II. and the Staff Manual respectively. Title pages will be prepared in manuscript.

Place	Date	Hour	Summary of Events and Information	Remarks and references to Appendices
ST NICHOLAS	5.12		The position of the Section so found was that a good one as was and howitzer knew up but to have a short out and many came which howe had been Ambulance cars but the Section has so far away rest to quick moves. the Ambulance was able are of fire. every act day. there was no rest here and the position there for long, knew was within the shell to water and the other fire everywhere but made every endeavour to cause as little hard as possible and not through the cats of ammo & the trucks load a duel and off to art a long survey to hard for the heavy arms ammunitions a true on the certains case. all the other howitzers batteries a hugh where distance from the Section, though to leave up shells & bombed to creatable occurred. One of how but him converted to Lilo no suffered to one of the fives to mal had been informed to find a help so a Car returning hist to a body from the Bayen - R.V.C. Connection of T.N.CO	

WAR DIARY / INTELLIGENCE SUMMARY

Army Form C. 2118.

29 Mobile Vety Section
17 Division. May 1917.

Place	Date	Hour	Summary of Events and Information	Remarks and references to Appendices
NICHOLAS			Out 10 men offered great assistance in evacuating	
"	17-31		animals not fit for the section's carry on to normal horse lines. Very few horses evacuated. As the cases were met with Seborrh. Skin & Glanders Culture test. Hundreds of cases of which were seen to be improving greatly. Section touched to not been at COUTERELLE. A flash	
"	31		No horse at any heart so that the great amount of traffic around Arras might be met with. On	
OUTERELLE	31		excellent Camp has been chosen at COUTERELLE and it	

Army Form C. 2118.

WAR DIARY 29 Mobile Vety Section

or

INTELLIGENCE SUMMARY. 17 Division May 1917

(Erase heading not required.)

Instructions regarding War Diaries and Intelligence Summaries are contained in F. S. Regs., Part II. and the Staff Manual respectively. Title pages will be prepared in manuscript.

Place	Date	Hour	Summary of Events and Information	Remarks and references to Appendices
BOUZERELLE	31.		Officers may commence care for sick horses.	
			During the month a system of forming Corps mobile Veterinary detachments was made while this and	
			was a VIII Corps 1 NCO and 2 men here have been away to form	
			the personnel for those Rest Units and left us to still	
			remain a Corps troops,	
			The system of making horses lspecial of these in twenties	
			was during the January was adopted speeds a	
			just excuses as animals could get a [speedier?]	
			while in the train. 17 Division "D" arranged that the	

A 5834 Wt. W4973/M687 750,000 8/16 D. D. & L. Ltd. Forms/C.2118/13.

WAR DIARY or INTELLIGENCE SUMMARY

Army Form C. 2118.

29th Battle Vet: Regt.
17th Khorasan
May 1917.

(Erase heading not required.)

Place	Date	Hour	Summary of Events and Information	Remarks and references to Appendices

Salonge Co. proceeded (in) 4 small patrol cars from the Section
moved off the track and as not the letter has no those
is last during transit have not heard time after
a short distance off the track is shelled out of the
during an excursion at times the 100 yds third Army.
evaded null head & marched to bivouac to hunt
and exposed to O.C. two persons at the moment
say that ammunition may be had off schemes not
to bivouac in the house of race depot they into rest
within the future time of rest
Wounded received 187. Russian, 2.
evacuated 185.

J.J. Hummel
Capt
O.C. 29 Bn V.S.

## WAR DIARY
INTELLIGENCE SUMMARY

Army Form C. 2118.

29 Mobile Veterinary Section

June 1917

Place	Date	Hour	Summary of Events and Information	Remarks and references to Appendices
COUTURELLE	1-22		The Section was at rest with Divison from 1st to 22nd. Since in an excellent Camp very little work was called for and the Section had a thorough rest from the hard work put in during the Battle of Arras. The Section was supplied with technical stores and personnel also. The Canto was a good one and good accommodation was found for men, horses and stores.	
COUTURELLE	22-30		Section marched to ANZIN near ARRAS and took over M.V.S of the 34th Division. Owing to the fact that the	
ANZIN			M.V.S of the 34th Division had not taken over the movement	

WAR DIARY or INTELLIGENCE SUMMARY

Army Form C. 2118.

29 Mobile Veterinary Section

June 1917.

2.

Place	Date	Hour	Summary of Events and Information	Remarks and references to Appendices
ANZIN	22-30		Site at ST NICHOLAS and that to 4th Division M.V.S. had taken possession it was lost to us. A great deal of work had been put in on this site & much improvement carried out. The site was in the centre of our horse transport and convenient to Anzac Station. A line fires was taken over at ANZIN there being no accommodation for here or stores. The Division had to be asked for assistance. Accommodation for men we had, stores and sick horses put up which was entering much labour to the very section showed late our own men much relieve and my improvements	

WAR DIARY or INTELLIGENCE SUMMARY

Army Form C. 2118.

29 Motor Amb'ce Convoy Station

June 1917

Place	Date	Hour	Summary of Events and Information	Remarks and references to Appendices

ANZIN

Wd and atta ched to the Anzin Stn to be for from two posts and Rail head. 135 Animals were admitted to the Section Sickness

129 were evacuated, 2 were destroyed and four were discharged Cured. Latrines all the crews here from Anzin.

In an Safe the remain in as being Alterations Established.

Anzin was used as Rail head and every convenience was given to the Section especially the facilities for obtaining from Supply picture time for carrying Animals for the List head.

P. Thirdell
Capt.
O.C. 29 Conv. S.

Army Form C. 2118.

WAR DIARY
or
INTELLIGENCE SUMMARY

29 Mobile Veterinary Section
17 Divisions

July 1917.

Vol 25

Place	Date	Hour	Summary of Events and Information	Remarks and references to Appendices
ANZAC	1-31 July		At Anjou Cant. Ordinary Section Routine attended to. Camp was improved as regards horse lines Cart horses, stables, guards etc. Forage Barn harness room hut etc. The Camp was enclosed by a wire fence and a hung hand was erected some little distance x the horse ins fences in three separate attendants (tro) for it and was necessary owing to the large numbers of mangs that were admitted from time to time during the month. Owing to attention of establishment a Staff-Sergeant was added to the Section and this to a.c section took on the veterinary charge of the 17 Ambulance Train	

Army Form C. 2118.

WAR DIARY
or
INTELLIGENCE SUMMARY. 29th Div. between Sectors
(Erase heading not required.) 17 Division

Place	Date	Hour	Summary of Events and Information	Remarks and references to Appendices
RN2LN	1-3 Sep		but the inspection of the front two trenches was very slight and with the fine weather conditions for the beneemed were excellent. Can't no quite ten holes and was obstance of wire were bad.	
			160 Arivols were rained for which 154 were executed 2 arrivols destroyed and to lines of communication 4 re-caved as cured. The greatest number of movements arrivals were many Cases, a small number of Children Cows and some artillery	

P.S. Rundel
Capt
OC 29 Int. Int. Sec.

WAR DIARY
or
INTELLIGENCE SUMMARY.

(Erase heading not required.)

Army Form C. 2118.

29 Mobile Vety Section
August 1917.

Vol 26

Place	Date	Hour	Summary of Events and Information	Remarks and references to Appendices
ANZIN	1-31 August		This has been an exceptionally quiet month, the Section having very little few sick animals to evacuate. 79 animals were received and were disposed of as follows. 76 Evacuated, two Returned to Units, one destroyed. The post-mortem on the destroyed animal revealed into enteritis of an advanced type with many lesions though the internal organs. No work was done towards making huts to store changes for the horses, and huts for the personnel stores as the section is to take over the buildings of the XVII Corps horse rest Camp when it closes down in September.	

J.P. Kennedy
Capt
O.C. 29 Mob. Vet. Sec.

WAR DIARY or INTELLIGENCE SUMMARY

29 Mobile Veterinary Section
17 Division

September 1917

Place	Date	Hour	Summary of Events and Information	Remarks and references to Appendices
ANZIN	1-9-17 to 15-9-17		At ANZIN Camp awaiting removal of Camp to two of Quintin across the road to XVII Corps Horse Rest Camp. The Section had the usual routine but to attend to for the first week, the horses being evacuated in small numbers a truck at the time. During the second week the O.C. and some of the Section personnel saw to the completion of the XVII Corps Horse Dip and Shephen Bath. The O.C. conveyed one of the Section Sergeants to the Horse Vet at MONDICOURT for a few days instruction prior to the opening of the XVII Corps Bath. The final preparations for the Bath having been made the Section moved to the site vacated by the XVII Corps Horse Rest Camp.	
RR AS.	16-9-17 to 25-9-17.		Section in position and for this period of 9 days a great deal of work was put in towards erection of winter quarters.	

WAR DIARY or INTELLIGENCE SUMMARY

Army Form C. 2118.

Instructions regarding War Diaries and Intelligence Summaries are contained in F. S. Regs., Part II. and the Staff Manual respectively. Title pages will be prepared in manuscript.

2/ 29 Mobile Vety Section

September 1917

O. Duncan

Place	Date	Hour	Summary of Events and Information	Remarks and references to Appendices
ARRAS	16-9-17		2 guns tent of cleaning up had to be done the Abris required	
	26-9-17		flagging. Cook stoves with permanent seed Tel chens erected, mess dining room, 2 harness room, hot and cold fittings for same, showers, a stove Room and Forge Room put up — all these are permanent structures and the section personnel worked very hard all day while light lasted to get the line to Quarters prepared. At the same time the VIII Corps Horse Dept Inspection Bath was dug & its lining running and to make the Bath a success meant its being run every day Thur 9 to the Bath 7 days successfully with out an accidents taking place. On the 24th the Bath was closed down for emptying out, cleaning and refixing with new mixture. During the working of the Bath my activities were hotly and these were later to be handed by CRE VIII Corps and new being attended to within the section on 25-9-17 — moved away on 25-9-17	

Army Form C. 2118.

WAR DIARY
or
INTELLIGENCE SUMMARY.

29 Mobile Veterinary Section
17th November

(Erase heading not required.)

Title pages September 1917

Place	Date	Hour	Summary of Events and Information	Remarks and references to Appendices
ARRAS	16-9-17 & 25-9-17		A Sergeant and 6 men left for a few days to instruct the incoming Mob. Vet. Section of 61st Division as to duties of Section. Standing pens for the retaining horses of the farm adjoining section were made accommodating with cover for over 100 animals formed but section moved before these pens could be effected. Amongst the effects of Mr Corps Horse Camp taken over was a Field Forge, Chaff Cutter & these were left in situ for use of incoming Mob. Vet. Sec. and succeeding sections.	
ARRAS — LE CAUROY	25-9-17		Section moved with Divisional to LE CAUROY is Rest area. Section left ARRAS at 9am and proceeded by tractor our Convoy to LE CAUROY arriving at 2 pm after having had a very good march.	
LE CAUROY	25-9-17 & 30-9-17		Section took over red site and New Horse Lines were completed first of. Section being overworked as refinew workstations.	
			93 animals were admitted for month. 91 animals evacuated to Field 89 Mob Vet Section. 2 animals returned to the unit.	9/S W. Wright Capt. C. 29 Mob Vet. Sec.

WAR DIARY or INTELLIGENCE SUMMARY

Army Form C. 2118.

2 Mounted Veterinary Section

October 1917.

Place	Date	Hour	Summary of Events and Information	Remarks and references to Appendices
Le Cauroy	1-4		Section in rest area at LE CAUROY. Refitting Section personnel and technical equipment. There no sick animals admitted.	
MECHURCH - PROVEN	4-5		Section entrained at MONDICOURT station en route for PROVEN at 1200 noon and arrived at PROVEN station PROVEN at 1200 that night. Section detrained and marched to camp. The position occupied by the outgoing section of the 20 Division was found untenable as all ten ts and shelters had been taken away by that unit. The Section finished at PARDO Camp on A.S.C. position and conferred with the NO. 4. Co. 17 DIVISIONAL TRAIN during our stay at PROVEN. There was no hut doing here for the free charge the animals was in Proven. The animals lying about stable area will ask 14 CORPS to O.C. hno	
PROVEN	5-11			

Army Form C. 2118.

WAR DIARY
or
INTELLIGENCE SUMMARY.
(Erase heading not required.)

29 Mobile Veterinary Section
October 1917

Place	Date	Hour	Summary of Events and Information	Remarks and references to Appendices
PROVEN	5-11		Instructions to take the Section over to Guiding Station in the forward area of the 14th Corps. The mobile section lines of the 29 Division were visited and found totally unsuitable. The lines were in a soft mud field some short distance from the Road side. The had no accommodation for men or stores. Having looked about a site was selected at ONDANK CABARET on the WOESTEN Road. This seemed accessible being near to the men and stores. A chalk pit from which a large amount had been taken was available and one situated down near flat able to hurt. A large number on high ground and are now used for horse lines as are opened straight up. A very good main Road.	
ONDANK	11-31		The section moved to on the 11th at 1300 hours and very soon the section settled in and lines were erected that day. Two sick horses were made over to the ELVERDINCHE Coll Road, the other new WELSH FARM Sheet 28. A.20.a. Central.	

WAR DIARY or INTELLIGENCE SUMMARY

Army Form C. 2118.

29 Mobile Veterinary Section

October 1917

Place	Date	Hour	Summary of Events and Information	Remarks and references to Appendices
ONSTANK	1/- 31		Animals were evacuated from the forward area as brought to the INTERNATIONAL CORNER by the MOBILE SECTION or to the remounts cleaning station. A great number of wounded and very lame animals were collected and the demands on the Mobile Ambulance was great so much so that extra assistance had to be given by the team of Mobile Ghants from the Mobile Brigade in the back area - now and then the Mobile Ambulance was used to clear animals were brought & taken by the signal station units and in such an inhaus too condition that they had to be taken to assistance of the front to proceed further. A great deal of good work was done by this area party both in rendering assistance from enemy bombs before the suffered casualties from enemy bombs before the section learnt to heed known that all men enemy raid limits from all Corps brought assistance	

WAR DIARY or INTELLIGENCE SUMMARY

Army Form C. 2118.

29/Mobile Veterinary Section

October 1917

Place	Date	Hour	Summary of Events and Information	Remarks and references to Appendices
ONSTANK	1-	3.0	and it was nearly 5 a.m. The horses were very hard hauled as after he was out about night clearing badly knocked animals & housing others & taking but to the station time for evacuation all the next two extra to over daily routine. The coming of the section by the Schone acting as Veterinary Clearing Station come had been hits as the body appeared animals had to wait here a few clays before the V.C.C. Station homed took th animals in - On one occasion 40 Animals all horses were here sent back to ONSTANK as their infected showed or confirmed heat were all animals showed here had a prepare and title of the V.C.C'S went all fine, also dug out with shelter where by action was in a much fired. Comes the section have been cleared every day much fewer horses has occurred and the conditions of the	

WAR DIARY
or
INTELLIGENCE SUMMARY.
(Erase heading not required.)

Army Form C. 2118.

Place	Date	Hour	Summary of Events and Information	Remarks and references to Appendices
			Animals embarked.	
			733 Animals have received all the animals from Divisional	
			693 have evacuated	
			27 Received from the Anvil	
			13 destroyed as being incurable. A large number	
			of animals have received that are not shown in our books	
			as when they have evacuated here it was often most advisable	
			to keep animals on/to more and get them to graze but	
			as they have had have get have in section and had the first	
			to go further. 80% of the Animals here have been cuts/punctures	
			by Aerial bombs. 10% have wounds of the feet. 5% Wounds	
			generally the run an or ability as a horse as injured.	
			On the departure of the 14 Corps Horses (a Cap) Cook took	
			D.S.O. wrote a letter of appreciation and thanks for the	
			good work done by the section in the forward area	

Army Form C. 2118.

WAR DIARY
or
INTELLIGENCE SUMMARY.

29th Wilts Wytsschaete Sector
October 1917.

(Erase heading not required.)

Place	Date	Hour	Summary of Events and Information	Remarks and references to Appendices
ONSTANC	1-31		The weather being very favourable Enemy bombing raids were a nightly occurrence and much damage was done to horse lines - A little shelling occurred heavy at times at opening & on DARK to Sector worked entirely for CORPS on later to Divisional front to Kiel area & for a few days to the line the Sector remained at its front and continued work & clearing its forward area.	

J.S. Newall
Capt R.E.
O/C 29th Wilts Coy

WAR DIARY or INTELLIGENCE SUMMARY

Army Form C. 2118.

29 Mobile Veterinary Section

NOVEMBER 1917

Place	Date	Hour	Summary of Events and Information	Remarks and references to Appendices
ONDANK.	1-30		During November the Section was acted as the Forward Mobile Collecting Station. Two Outposts were kept at ELVERDINGHE and at HOSPITAL FARM H.20.A central as Veterinary Aid hosts, that contained Horse Lines as all the animals as to the forward area were received. The 1st & 14th Corps continuing the same Veterinary Arrange had to do was to 1st + 14th Corps. The Section was not cleared daily as it should have been and large numbers of animals were kept indoors long especially gun shot wound cases. Ambulance trains was again heavy — the front with a relay of horses going all day long. Four do do to middle of the month but gradually slackened off owing to the withdrawal from this front of many divisions so to last declared up to each of the Mobile Sections	

Army Form C. 2118.

WAR DIARY
or
INTELLIGENCE SUMMARY.

30 Mobile Veterinary Section
November 1917.

(Erase heading not required.)

Place	Date	Hour	Summary of Events and Information	Remarks and references to Appendices
ON TREK	1-30		of the Corps here & dried to carry on in their own country and never into their own crossed country to the rear of the other two mobile sections being so far behind that the run down of the hoof feet to us as we advanced. The system of evacuation the formal of evacuation adopted by the Corps was a bad one – Animals were evacuated once a week and long train being made up to evacuate for the Corps from INTERNATIONAL CORNER, starting to travel for days and after 10 days without our 100 sick animals living in the open and starving to death have was the result for the section as its entering trains of the animals in such conditions was very arduous and as nearly all the cases to the front half of the month were horses & mules it needed considerable force to the first half of the month were, Animals	

WAR DIARY
INTELLIGENCE SUMMARY

Army Form C. 2118.

29 Mobile Vety Section

November 1917

Place	Date	Hour	Summary of Events and Information	Remarks and references to Appendices
ONDANK	1	30	showed to be evacuated at once and not kept waiting long in mobile vety sections. During our spare time staring for 25 horses was erected and completed while another stable to hold 65 animals was under course of erection and nearing completion. Sleeping accommodation for Horsemen was built and extended so that each man had a wire bed. A harness room and Anti-horse for Kitchen, Saddle and Store room also erected. An old farm house in the Cmpt was done up and afforded cover & shelter for the Section horses. A deal of work was put in to make the Cmpt a permanent home to go into and everything we have built can fort able. When this evacuation went out Horses are for 3 weeks the section was kept on the line waiting.	

WAR DIARY or INTELLIGENCE SUMMARY

Army Form C. 2118.

4 Mobile Vety Section   November 1917

Place	Date	Hour	Summary of Events and Information	Remarks and references to Appendices
ON TRNK	Nov 1-30		As to report of Vet Corps. There was hardly any bombing carried out by the enemy at a near the section except for one night. Enemy shells fell almost on the section during the last two days of the month but no casualties occurred.	
			Admitted Sick 719 Animals	
			Evacuated 673 "	
			Returned Cured 18 "	
			Died 2 "	
			Destroyed 8 "	
			Remaining 20 "	
			Now as for the past 14 days of the month we had the chief mirage with D elivity reck. In the last 14 days when heat was dealt becomes was the	

WAR DIARY

2 9th Mble Vety Section

November 1917

Army Form C. 2118.

Place	Date	Hour	Summary of Events and Information	Remarks and references to Appendices
ONDANK		1-30	Was the chief cause of head off. Cellulitis was & proportion to the numbers of animals received very small. A large number of cases of Ophthalmia in heavy draught horses and a few mange – the mange cases were not an at Glorg Standing. The numbers of animals from the Divisions was considerably less.	

J.J. Kinney
O.C. 29 Mbl. Vet. Section

1/12/17

WAR DIARY
or
INTELLIGENCE SUMMARY

Army Form C. 2118.

29 Mobile Veterinary Section
17 Divison

December 1917

Place	Date	Hour	Summary of Events and Information	Remarks and references to Appendices
ONDRANK	Dec. 1-5.		During period December 1 to 5 the Section was still found M.V.S. for 19th Corps and during this time the new stable for 140 horses was almost completed as well as a new forage barn. 113 animals admitted for treatment. 22 have been found ally Gun Shot Wounds. Animals were shod shod of in wood bay.	VM 30
PROVEN	5-7.		Section moved out to Back area as Division coming out of the line being relieved by the 2nd Division M.V.S.	
ESQUELBECQ	7.		Section moved to ESQUELBECQ a staging area on way to ZUYTKERKE. off to CHLAIS-STOMER Road. The H.Q. transport forming Section for the march to ZUYTKERKE.	
ZUYTKERKE	8-13		Section in rest area. Good Billets for men was made but the accomodation for the horses was but fair. Weather conditions bad and a Great flood in the Ware River	

WAR DIARY or INTELLIGENCE SUMMARY

Army Form C. 2118.

2 Mobile Veterinary Section

December 1917

(Erase heading not required.)

Place	Date	Hour	Summary of Events and Information	Remarks and references to Appendices
ZUTKERKE	8-12		The collecting of animals left by units in rest area the usual accompanying task when a mobile section goes out to rest was made and long distances had to be made.	
EPERLECQUE	13		The rest area being changed to another bivouac near the section marched to EPERLECQUES and on the way was halted and made to stand to, 6 also were here for the section to go into billets at EPERLECQUE and arrival from 6 also to move by train at 13 hours from Zuo time. A string 1/20 horn dead animals two trains (one cars were got rid of during the 12 hours trip to 6 23 VETERINARY HOSPITAL a distance of about 10 kilometres each way	
ST OMER- BAUPOME	14 – 15		Section left to entraining and entrained at 9pm at ST OMER and travelled all night to BAUPOME arriving that place at 10am next day when the section marched to	

Army Form C. 2118.

WAR DIARY
or
INTELLIGENCE SUMMARY.

(Erase heading not required.)

29 Mobile Veterinary Section

December 1917

Place	Date	Hour	Summary of Events and Information	Remarks and references to Appendices
ACHIET-LE-PETIT.	1/7 to 15		ACHIET-LE-PETIT where H.Q.(Mobile Vet Section) H.Q. was located. Lets found for men and horses includes a shed. The section standing to during the few days here the weather got very cold and snow fell for two days, operations of hunting for the men being trying. A few sick animals were taken in and they were brought to section to section in the time.	
ACHIET-LE-PETIT	15 to 23			
HAPLINCOURT	23 to 31		Section marched to HAPLINCOURT having been ordered there by 5th CORPS. The section horses and transport had to be prepared with frost cogs and roughing of shoes for the track which was made without mishap - a few sick were brought along. A good billet for all was found. Stables being unavailable. Section soon settled down to work and reception of sick horses begun, but no light and I don't expect much to do for the section	

A5834 Wt.W4973/M687 750,000 8/16 D.D.&L.Ltd. Forms/C.2118/13.

WAR DIARY
INTELLIGENCE SUMMARY

Army Form C. 2118.

29 Mobile Veterinary Section

December 1917

Place	Date	Hour	Summary of Events and Information	Remarks and references to Appendices
HARLINCOURT	23		In this section there are a number of Sections here to help to the evacuation of animals. During the last week the weather has most severe and much snow fell. Conditions of work were hard but the men worked Cheerfully. It is unfortunate that the Section did not have its long rest in the ST OMER area as it was held awaiting to the hard and trying work put in from Oct 9th to October 5th while the Corps has attacking on the PASSCHENDAELE RIDGE. On leaving the 19th Corps to Cope sent a letter of approval to the A.H. & Q.M.G of 17 Division and hoping our next section while the Division was out at Rest to the late V.A.O.	

Animals Received — Animals Evacuated 168 Died — Destroyed 4
Horses 39 Mules 36
Animals Evacuated from 17 Division = Horses 152 Mules 16

Army Form C. 2118.

WAR DIARY
or
INTELLIGENCE SUMMARY.

(Erase heading not required.)

29 Mobile Veterinary Section
January 1917

Vol 31

Instructions regarding War Diaries and Intelligence Summaries are contained in F.S. Regs., Part II. and the Staff Manual respectively. Title pages will be prepared in manuscript.

Place	Date	Hour	Summary of Events and Information	Remarks and references to Appendices
HAPLINCOURT	January 1-31		The Section remained at HAPLINCOURT all the month acting as a collecting station for the V. Corps. Work was very light and admissions of sick and wounded few. All animals were evacuated to 34 Mobile Vety Section at ETRICOURT which was the V. Corps Veterinary Casualty Clearing Station. 4 men from this unit being detached to it to act as conducting parties to the Base. Owing to the light nature of the work a great deal of building and improvements was made to the Camp. A long stance was covered in and a standing hall of brick rubble. The stance was revetted by means of a hurt of earth as a protection against bombs. A hutern wagon hope was laso constructed	

Army Form C. 2118.

WAR DIARY
or
INTELLIGENCE SUMMARY.

29 Mobile Veterinary Section

January 1918

(Erase heading not required.)

Place	Date	Hour	Summary of Events and Information	Remarks and references to Appendices
Plinsoves Farm	1-31		Mens Cook house and drying room hut out also Officers quarters. Road to huts construction from Stable to new Road. This is the third Camp constructed by this section so far this Winter and it so happens that once the Camp is made secure and comfortable for personnel & animals the Section is moved further afield.	
			150 animals been admitted.	
			154 animals evacuated	
			2 Destroyed	
			4 Returned as Cured to units.	
			24 animals only belonged to 19 Divisions as the cause of wastage was Ophthalmia the other cases being 9/75 & 97.5 Wingel as usual heth.	

Army Form C. 2118.

WAR DIARY
or
INTELLIGENCE SUMMARY
29 Mobile Veterinary Section
February 1918

(Erase heading not required.)

Instructions regarding War Diaries and Intelligence Summaries are contained in F. S. Regs., Part II. and the Staff Manual respectively. Title pages will be prepared in manuscript.

Place	Date	Hour	Summary of Events and Information	Remarks and references to Appendices
APLINCOURT.	1-28.		During the month of February 1918 the Mobile Section continued at APLINCOURT. The work for the period was of the ordinary Routine nature and evacuations were not heavy. The principal diseases for which animals were evacuated were Mange and Debility and some cases of Ophthalmia. The mange and debility occurred amongst aged animals of units other than this division. Forty remounts that were drawn from a Remount train at BAUPOME had a case of Contagious Stomatitis amongst the Remounts drawn by the 47 Division. The 17 Divisional Artillery and Infantry drew the Remounts, Artillery having 35 the Infantry the Rest. Steps were at once taken to isolate these animals. The Artillery Remounts were several up to	

Army Form C. 2118.

29 Mobile Veterinary Section

February 1918

WAR DIARY
or
INTELLIGENCE SUMMARY

(Erase heading not required.)

Place	Date	Hour	Summary of Events and Information	Remarks and references to Appendices
			29 Brigade R.F.A. while the Infantry Reserves were located at the Mobile Section the division finding Sick attended to who were kept as a horsed detachable at the end of the relative period no stores nor having occurred the Reserves were sent to duty. Improvements to new hand to Section, a new harness room hut etc. A large piece of ground was forced in for purpose of burning bespoke. A small space for hothouse cases is in the course function. 140 horses and 26 mules have evacuated. One horse was destroyed. 90 animals were evacuated from the division suffering chiefly from debility being aged animals.	

W.S. Kennedy Capt.
2-3-18.

WAR DIARY or INTELLIGENCE SUMMARY

Army Form C. 2118.

29 Mobile Veterinary Section
June 1918 17th Division

Place	Date	Hour	Summary of Events and Information	Remarks and references to Appendices
MARLINCOURT	1-21		At Marlincourt attending to routine work. Work being light and all animals evacuated to V. Corps Veterinary Evacuating Clearing Station near Etrican. Additional improvements made to horse camp and a large piece of ground was fenced in to make a paddock and no horses to be horsed. On morning of 21st at 5 am a intense bombardment was opened on Marlincourt and surrounding area and enemy fire kept up all day with very heavy high explosive. The first dump was set alight. The section horse lines were hit. The hits have ranged from 77's Minnies. The section made a dug out for wounded and carried on ordinary routine while a heavy fire was kept up. 30 wounded animals were evacuated in the afternoon to the V.C.C. station as at 5.00 pm the section packed up and moved our country to Beaulencourt in a orderly manner, bringing along a small string of wounded animals - only one casualty was left behind, it was unable to move and was destroyed. The section proceeded to join some horse lines near Havincourt and all stores to the Mobile Video An Hop. Hospital where we got supplementary	

C.P.
(A8004) Wt. W1711 P2-31 725/500 3/17 Sch 32 Forms/C.2118/14
D. H. & L., London, E.C.

Army Form C. 2118.

29th/the Veterinary Section
March 1918.

WAR DIARY
or
INTELLIGENCE SUMMARY.
(Erase heading not required.)

Instructions regarding War Diaries and Intelligence Summaries are contained in F. S. Regs., Part II. and the Staff Manual respectively. Title pages will be prepared in manuscript.

Place	Date	Hour	Summary of Events and Information	Remarks and references to Appendices
BEAULENCOURT	21–23		I did wire collected on Bapaume – Lemare Road and section stayed up a number of horses from our armies has received but had to be discharged. A number were found lost they have collected and issued to the demands of transports. On the morning of 23rd Big Guns came of Bapaume and horses had to be vacated to a place within Beaulencourt whilst on the morn rains the enemy put heavy tear shrapnel over us. The Section then went at Beaulencourt had to be vacated as the 79 B at R.P.M came to its one camp and advanced and the Section to proceed at once to be sent to the 174th Divisions train. Camp at Beaulencourt was shelled while we were there. Orders were that we should at 5.30 a pm and set to be sent at 900 section picketing to the others – horsed American were brought along with Section on a continuous line.	
LE SARS LA BOISELLE HENENCOURT	24		At noon Section was ordered back to LA BOISELLE and proceeded on old front line and stated to be moved at 4. PM to Henencourt. Our attempt on route we were halted for great part and a half owing to congestion of traffic and	

D. D. & L., London, E.C.
(A8004) Wt. W1771/M2118 750,000 5/17 Sch: 53 Forms/C2118/14

WAR DIARY
or
INTELLIGENCE SUMMARY.

Army Form C. 2118.

29 Mobile Veterinary Section

March 1918

Place	Date	Hour	Summary of Events and Information	Remarks and references to Appendices
LESARS - LABOISSELLE - HENENCOURT	2nd		It was with difficulty I got the big things forward here though, I had although during the evening as that neighbouring to the congestion of traffic and the enemy bombing and machine gunning horses here lost their animals. Helped at Henencourt and convoyed to 3rd Corps horse as to heads and horses and hauled them over to the 3rd Corps V.C.C.S.	
HENENCOURT - CONTAY			Marched from the back to Contay and again picked up animals and started to - Evernies to 5th Corps V.C.C.S other animals that had been admitted the V.CCS being at Vadencourt.	
CONTAY - ACHEUX - VCHEVILLERS	26		Orders to move horses from Contay for fear of being cut off. Marched again with Divisional Transport and rear of Divisional Ammunition Column, passed through Varchonvillers which villages they were shelling as we passed through, also Louvencourt. Had to Acheux at 10.00 pm on side of road near station. Got to shelter falling and buildings new village whilst the Bochus here were bombarding and Bochie sunniped fanatics to evacuate occurred to the ceiling at 12oc midnight as we were	

Army Form C. 2118.

29th Mobile Veterinary Section

March 1918

WAR DIARY
or
INTELLIGENCE SUMMARY.
(Erase heading not required.)

Instructions regarding War Diaries and Intelligence Summaries are contained in F. S. Regs., Part II. and the Staff Manual respectively. Title pages will be prepared in manuscript.

Place	Date	Hour	Summary of Events and Information	Remarks and references to Appendices
CONTAY ACHEUX	26		Struck tents again and pushed on to Puchevillers with horses - he marched all night and horses and him here tied out. Received a few sick and wounded.	
PUCHEVILLERS Val de MAISON	27		At noon moved to Septonville with the H.Q. again Standing by. Received a number of sick and wounded.	
	28		The two days (26 & 27) at Septonville were badly needed as section here tired out and men too tired full opportunity of the rest. Evacuated horses all the sick animals to V.C.C.S.	
VAL de MAISON MIRVAUX	29		On two being held he moved to MIRVAUX returning towards the front. Section in charge with 2nd Lt Riches was found here to find site for horse lines. Repaired to lines at once horse lines.	
MIRVAUX	30-31		Overhauled section repaired harness, brushes etc awaiting themselves of the quiet rest at Mirvaux. A number of Gunner animals received and evacuated to 7th Corps V.C.C.S at Flesselles.	

Army Form C. 2118.

WAR DIARY
or
INTELLIGENCE SUMMARY.
(Erase heading not required.)

29th Mobile Veterinary Section

March 1918

Place	Date	Hour	Summary of Events and Information	Remarks and references to Appendices
MIRVAUX	30-31		The Section had a very hard and trying time and it was astonishing during the bombardment of Franvillers with direct hits that we suffered no casualties as both the horses and the stables were full and round the Section stables. It was difficult to be able to get all to sit and horses away that day. The Section behaved splendidly. The night marching was very trying specially looking after the sick horses all our sick was cleared a number were shot as they were incurable. Animals received. 124. Animals evacuated. 98. Animals destroyed. 14. Animals received. 12.	

J.S. Kunkel
Capt.
a/c 29 M.V.S.
31/3/18

Army Form C. 2118.

WAR DIARY
INTELLIGENCE SUMMARY.
29 Mobile Veterinary Section
April 1918

(Erase heading not required.)

Instructions regarding War Diaries and Intelligence Summaries are contained in F. S. Regs., Part II. and the Staff Manual respectively. Title pages will be prepared in manuscript.

Place	Date	Hour	Summary of Events and Information	Remarks and references to Appendices
MIRVAUX	1-4		at MIRVAUX standing to and carrying on routine duty of section. Only a few horses being admitted.	
FLESSELLES	4-11		Section moved to FLESSELLES with horses to a camp but selected on HAOURS Road there having picketed a straw barn being found for the personnel. Advantage was taken of the stay at FLESSELLES to equit better stores and personnel, had no light a few camp ovens he admitted. As there was completely overhead and defensive due to the retirement advanced.	
PUCHEVILLERS	11-20		Section moved back to to line halting temporarily at PUCHEVILLERS village for the night 11th-12th and proceeding to a camp on a sunken road off the PUCHE-VILLERS - TOUTENCOURT Road. A good site was selected and the sunken road afforded good cover from the winds and enemy bombing as well as offer during great	

(A804) Wt. W2771/M2 31 750,000 5/17 **Sch. 52** Forms/C2118/14

17

Army Form C. 2118.

29 Mobile Veterinary Section
April 1918

Vol 34

WAR DIARY
or
INTELLIGENCE SUMMARY.
(Erase heading not required.)

Place	Date	Hour	Summary of Events and Information	Remarks and references to Appendices
BONNEVILLERS	11-20		Good standing for horses. Sub to provide for themselves. Owing to grouping together of Divisions the Section proceeded to ARQUEVES and a good camp was selected on the TROEUVES - VAUCHELLES Road. A small copse to a harbour afforded a good camping ground. Subs being provided for Section stores personnel. They are being run without any subject to every gun fire. The Section will be no ready to move that short notice.	
ARQUEVES	20-30		Animals evacuated 109. of the division 10 were evacuated destroyed cured. Evacuations by Road to DOULLENS E.V. Corps Veterinary Evacuation Station and are from fit Reserves. But evacuees conveyed by Section Horse and Motor Ambulance of the V. Corps.	

Army Form C. 2118.

WAR DIARY
or
INTELLIGENCE SUMMARY.
29 Mobile Veterinary Section
April 1918
(Erase heading not required.)

Instructions regarding War Diaries and Intelligence Summaries are contained in F. S. Regs., Part II. and the Staff Manual respectively. Title pages will be prepared in manuscript.

Place	Date	Hour	Summary of Events and Information	Remarks and references to Appendices
ARQUEVES		20.30	Looking to animals no due Chiefly to lice that worn do and the blistering and cracking of animal bodies & due to the effect of mustard Gas. There was no contagious or infectious disease. Date of mobilization of Section 29-4-15 proceeded overseas. 15.7.15.	

J.R. Kennel
Capt & ?
OC 29 Mob Vet Sec

WAR DIARY or INTELLIGENCE SUMMARY

Army Form C. 2118.

29 Mobile Veterinary Section

May 1918

Place	Date	Hour	Summary of Events and Information	Remarks and references to Appendices
ARQUEVES.	1-31.		Section throughout the month at the ARQUEVES. Capts. White the changes who is in the line. Section has been straining in each training to strange at one horse patient. Reduction in the establishment of Section no more. The Staff-Sergeant and one man is is required. Two additions we due to the formation of the Veterinary Evacuation Station appointed to each Corps, for sick and wounded being evacuated daily to Evacuation Station by road. The formation of the Evacuation Stations has made it obvious Veterinary textbook based practice as the horse line no longer of big numbers of animals on the line with but a few attendants. The work of the Section has also been lessened with the removal that have	

Army Form C. 2118.

WAR DIARY
or
INTELLIGENCE SUMMARY.

29 Mobile Veterinary Section
May 1918

(Erase heading not required.)

Place	Date	Hour	Summary of Events and Information	Remarks and references to Appendices
ARQUES	1-31		Attention can now be paid to [illegible] and to horses do [illegible]. No important [illegible] have [illegible] notice and [illegible] for no serious [illegible] known. 144 animals now admitted 137 Evacuated to No. 6 Veterinary Evacuation Station 6 Cases sent on to [illegible] 1 Died but has been [illegible] infection of stomach. 3 Remain under treatment. W.P. Kunkel Capt. OC 29 Mob. Vet. Sec.	

Army Form C. 2118.

WAR DIARY 29 Mobile Veterinary Section
or
INTELLIGENCE SUMMARY. June 1918

Vol 3

Place	Date	Hour	Summary of Events and Information	Remarks and references to Appendices
ARQUEVES.	June 1-23		Section at ARQUEVES attending to ordinary routine duty. Section prepared to move at the hours notice. Ordinary cases for evacuation have received aid for period 1-23 little to make mention of.	
HERISSART.	23-30		Section moved with Division to rest area near HERISSART a site being selected on a sunken road between HERISSART and TOUTENCOURT. The sunken road afforded excellent cover for the men and horses and very little bivouac had to be attended to the bivouac of reserve to for the tents and horse lines, this neighbourhood is visited nightly by enemy aircraft the section while in Rest area is prepared to move at half at one hours notice for the vicinity at HERISSART and was at times heavily shelled by enemy aeroplanes hombs inflicted on Ammo dumps by enemy aeroplane bombs a number of animals were killed — to below shown Sample	

Army Form C. 2118.

29 Mobile Veterinary Section

June 1918

WAR DIARY
or
INTELLIGENCE SUMMARY

(Erase heading not required.)

Instructions regarding War Diaries and Intelligence Summaries are contained in F. S. Regs., Part II. and the Staff Manual respectively. Title pages will be prepared in manuscript.

Place	Date	Hour	Summary of Events and Information	Remarks and references to Appendices
HERISSART	23-30		And looking the Shins to the Race.	
			139 Animals were admitted and disposed of as follows:-	
			Evacuated to 5th Corps Evacuating Station, 139 animals	
			Destroyed as incurable, 2 animals	
			Discharged as cured to units - 9 animals	
			Remaining are animal.	
			121 Animals evacuated from Division (17th)	

J J Kunkel
Capt.
1-7-19 O 29 Mob. Vet. Sec.

Army Form C. 2118.

29 Mobile Veterinary Section

July 1918

WAR DIARY
or
INTELLIGENCE SUMMARY.

(Erase heading not required.)

Place	Date	Hour	Summary of Events and Information	Remarks and references to Appendices
HERISSART	1-31 July		The Section remained at HERISSART and did not move from the area now retained as the Mobile Veterinary Sector.	
			9th 10th Divisions asked to be allowed stay on at TOTENCOURT and as the distance between the two sections was only half a mile this was started on at HERISSART. The Cinema is an ideal summer one as on a training ground for the trenches where sick animals come to hand and at times to graze. The broken wood have been thinned as advance afford excellent protection from the attacks of enemy bombing. Opportunity was taken of the presence of a good rifle range for the men to practise and shooting matches were arranged to encourage the men - Sand bag and nail and horse became quite efficient. During the month ordinary routine work was attended to.	(see over)

Army Form C. 2118.

Instructions regarding War Diaries and Intelligence Summaries are contained in F. S. Regs., Part II. and the Staff Manual respectively. Title pages will be prepared in manuscript.

29 Mobile Veterinary Section

WAR DIARY
or
INTELLIGENCE SUMMARY.
(Erase heading not required.)

July 1918

Place	Date	Hour	Summary of Events and Information	Remarks and references to Appendices
MERRIS ART	1-31 July		LAVICOGNE & to Corps Evacuating Station. Animals being despatched to road to LAVICOGNE & to Corps Evacuating Station. Animals were sent in the early morning so that they were not put to hard work in the dust roads on the return from this duty. Our horses from sheer exhaustion have also been the heritage of being Debilitas amongst old animals of th Artillery. There were 3 mange. 158 animals were admitted and discharged as follows:— Evacuated 154 Cured 2 Died or destroyed nil Remaining under treatment 2 134 horses and 20 mules have admitted 36 animals were fit for the Army in.	

J. S. Russell
29 Mobile VSection

17

Army Form C. 2118.

WAR DIARY
or
INTELLIGENCE SUMMARY.

29th Divisional Veterinary Section

August 1918

WO 38

(Erase heading not required.)

Instructions regarding War Diaries and Intelligence Summaries are contained in F.S. Regs., Part II. and the Staff Manual respectively. Title pages will be prepared in manuscript.

Place	Date	Hour	Summary of Events and Information	Remarks and references to Appendices
August HERISSART	-8th		Section in HERISSART in Rest area with Division. Period ordinary routine work was attended to.	
HERISSART	8th		Section marched to rear of Divisional Artillery to Australian Corps near Corbie. A night march was made and section bivouaced on banks of Somme River at BLANGY-TRONVILLE for the remainder of night and next day.	
BLANGY-TRONVILLE	9-10		Moved to DAOURS and used to manage & go forward with the divisions - Evacuate to Australian Veterinary Evacuation Station a few horses with minor ailments.	
DAOURS	10-13		Marched afternoon to near HAMELET but owing to congestion of transports in this area moved the section to a rise in a area from here and again here bivouaced in orchard. Whilst at FOUILLOY the Commander to the Division was slight	
FOUILLOY	13		FOUILLOY and secured a very good site	

WAR DIARY
or
INTELLIGENCE SUMMARY.
(Erase heading not required.)

Army Form C. 2118.

Place	Date	Hour	Summary of Events and Information	Remarks and references to Appendices
FOUILLOY	13–18		A large number of Ambulance Cases having occurred to the Australian V.E.S. has moved to CORBIE from evening 13th. Clear evening as the distance was too short a one.	
FOUILLOY	18		The Ambulance having come out the Station marched to the 50th Infantry Bde. front at 11.30pm and marched to new aid at HERRISART – The march took all night and was an unexpected one.	
HERRISART	18–23		At HERRISART with Ambulance at rest – Every ambulance devoted much attention to the comfort of patients. The ambulance to Ammiens very few.	
HERRISART – ACHEUX	9pm		The Ambulance going into action the Station was brought forward to ACHEUX. bath Res Ambulance #8 and stood to for the day.	
ACHEUX – ENGLEBELMER	24–27		Stood to attack ENGLEBELMER – 4 did ammts from the artillery only being received.	
ENGLEBELMER – AVELUY	27, 9.30		At AVELUY where a small number of wounded arrived. Infantry transport had a ————	

Army Form C. 2118.

WAR DIARY
or
INTELLIGENCE SUMMARY.
(Erase heading not required.)

2/2 Mobile Veterinary Section
August 1916

Place	Date	Hour	Summary of Events and Information	Remarks and references to Appendices
AVELUY – MARTINPUICH	30	–	Received late orders to move at half an hour's notice. Section moved at 6.00 pm to MARTIN PUICH & from thence to OC. new formed advanced aid for sick & lame horses. Arrived at about 9 pm.	
MARTINPUICH	30-31		Standing to but doing veterinary work every a few animals were received during the day. During this month especially towards the later half a great deal of marching had to be done and section had to be kept mobile. The section cleared the sick daily and by arranging F.S. trucks horses as well as the first animals went by walking. F.S. trucks horses as well as the first animals sent by the first crews came to get away during the nights or early mornings and these were the sections for lunch. Owing to the OC unit having to perform the Ypres FD duties at Amman HQ owing to the absence of FD doctors from the 21-31st there arising a lot of section work there was no arrangements for the section could be attended to alone as also to return to Office of Divisional or APM's covers during the time but with the transport & ambulance during the advance covering the the big advance to Chinoso Arrow – the Australian Corps advance by B.X.ay Sect. was employed in English advance on LE TRANSLOY & in evacuation was deeply committed in the amount & work done at over & and the	

WAR DIARY
or
INTELLIGENCE SUMMARY.

(Erase heading not required.)

Army Form C. 2118.

Ypres-Volyhens
August 1917

Place	Date	Hour	Summary of Events and Information	Remarks and references to Appendices
MARTINPUICH	30-31		Animals were exposed to shell fire and bombs. The Veterinary arrangements of the Cavalry Corps have issued as to the V.E.S. and its advanced post both in close touch with us. The same applies to the V. Corps V.E.S. except that an advanced post for the front area should have been brought forward. 118 Animals have been admitted (about 101 men horses) 1 Division passed one destroyed and 10 discharged cured.	

D. S. Kinkead
Capt
R. S. Vet. Corps. N. O i/c

WAR DIARY
INTELLIGENCE SUMMARY

Army Form C. 2118.

29 Mobile Veterinary Section

Title pages SEPTEMBER 1918

Vol. 39

Place	Date	Hour	Summary of Events and Information	Remarks and references to Appendices
MARTINPUICH	1-2		At MARTINPUICH with the Divisional H.Q. Section standing by ready to move at one hours notice. Sect was evacuating to AVELUY to No. 5 Veterinary Evacuating Station.	
MARTINPUICH / BEAULENCOURT	2nd		Section marched in rear of First Line Transport and with Divisional H.Q. to a similar rear area outside BEAULENCOURT and currently occupies the same area as the Section retired on March 23rd. An excellent camp was made at Beaulencourt the Brigade H.Q. of the German General VON DIETENBETHEM being accommodated. Excellent billets for the horses were being found.	
BEAULENCOURT	2-17		Section throughout performing ordinary routine. Section has prepared to hand over at sudden notice owing to the N.V.S. Evacuating Station moving to Beaulencourt, which delivered to hand over by Cart to Hut Unit on 9-9-18 and moved to an adjoining Section road have been left during our stay in this Camp.	
LECHELLE	17-30		On 17th Section was attached to LECHELLE and a Camp was pitched outside the Village on the ETRICOURT road. As the Section was the only one to meet the Cavalry Regiment subject to this time. The camp was attached to the last week cavalry from coming up to the last week	

WAR DIARY / INTELLIGENCE SUMMARY

Army Form C. 2118.

29 Mobile Veterinary Section

September 1918

Place	Date	Hour	Summary of Events and Information	Remarks and references to Appendices
LECHELLE		17-30	Of the month the changes have been out of the line and kept no weight. During the period for this service (for this service) the Mobile Section remained with Train H.Q. (A.S.C.) and in close proximity to new "B" H.Q. - This proved an invaluable arrangement as communications being always to the fort it is not necessary as that the Lane went by means of the Cavalry Gallopers. The Section being time enough found and to keep up with "B" H.Q. the Section was in close proximity to front line trans-port and of bring sick and wounded animals down the cattle as to let them free to travel. On the 14-9-18 am the unit sent to assist the Capt. I.V. Turston A.V.C. and officer in so need as for the homeless from the relief was no necessity do to the difficulty of Keeping a front with units. Wherever arriving force with units. Wherever 29 Mobile returned to ROEUX N/S on 8-9-18 Gallopers a daylight Experiment an Ambulance taken at the Amb. with the exception of horses a tent floor were to gregarious condition of the gear + the Ambulance taken into work the follow.	

D.D. & L., London, E.C.
(A502) Wt. W1771/M2031 750v.99 5/17 Sch. 52 Forms C2...0/14

Army Form C. 2118.

WAR DIARY
or
INTELLIGENCE SUMMARY.

29 Mobile Veterinary Section

(Erase heading not required.)

September 1918

Instructions regarding War Diaries and Intelligence Summaries are contained in F. S. Regs., Part II. and the Staff Manual respectively. Title pages will be prepared in manuscript.

Place	Date	Hour	Summary of Events and Information	Remarks and references to Appendices
LECHELLE	17	7.30.	And it afforded great relief in helping to clear the numerous first cases that occurs when the division is in action. Jam is attached to the RO & R.M.S 17 Division for the last advance and is given during its advance. Casualties were principally from enemy gun fire though enemy bombs accounted for a good number. There was no contagious or Infectious disease had. 246 Animals were admitted. 239 Animals evacuated of which 207 were of 17 Division. 2 Destroyed. 5. Remained no cured.	

J.E. Knell
Capt
OC 29 Mobile Vety Section

Army Form C. 2118.

WAR DIARY
or
INTELLIGENCE SUMMARY.

(Erase heading not required.)

29 Mobile Veterinary Section
October 1918

Place	Date	Hour	Summary of Events and Information	Remarks and references to Appendices
LECHELLE	1-5		At LECHELLE with Divisional Reinforcements awaiting horses duty.	
LECHELLE – FINS.	5.		Section marched to FINS with 19 Riding horses. Train HQ and Stores by.	
FINS	5-8		At FINS standing to and as Evacuating Station moved to FINS Stn and handed over animals, become shortly handed our them only a few animals were received at FINS.	
FINS – WALINCOURT	8-		Marched to BANTEUX and halted on the East side of Canal on road available atop the Section marched through L GOUZEAUCOURT, GONNELIER BANTEUX. At Banteux had a midday halt and watered and fed. Section one to dead to WALINCOURT marching via BANTOUZELLE and FRM de MONTECOUVEZ and across country to WALINCOURT where a camp was pitched that evening in a Sunken road.	

Army Form C. 2118.

WAR DIARY
or
INTELLIGENCE SUMMARY.
(Erase heading not required.)

29 Mobile Veterinary Section

October 1918

2.

Place	Date	Hour	Summary of Events and Information	Remarks and references to Appendices
WALINCOURT – MONTIGNY	9		Section marched to MONTIGNY and took up that village. A number of sick animals found here, these were put up section as the Evacuating officer was too far behind to be able to get the animals away that unit had moved up.	
MONTIGNY	9-23		At MONTIGNY attending to animals sent down.	
MONTIGNY – INCHY	23		Section marched with Divisional HQ to INCHY.	
INCHY	23-27		Billets for men and a large stable were obtained at INCHY. New Section came into action. Routine.	
INCHY – NEUVILLY	27		Section marched with Divn. HQ to NEUVILLY a disused factory being utilized for use as stables.	
NEUVILLY	27-31		Section at NEUVILLY. 188 animals been admitted. Evacuated. 6 discharged. 14 remained to units lost "	

W. Leonard
Lt.
a/o 29 MVS

Army Form C. 2118.

29 Mobile Veterinary Section
November 1918

WAR DIARY
or
INTELLIGENCE SUMMARY.

(Erase heading not required.)

Place	Date	Hour	Summary of Events and Information	Remarks and references to Appendices
NEUVILLY	1-5.		Ordinary routine work was attached to until the reporter that the section was made a dump for the front line of the other divisions on route to H.Q.S. Veterinary Evacuating Station.	
NEUVILLY	5.		Section marched via VENDEGIES-au-BOIS to low divisional H.Q at POIX-du-NORD. An excellent farm house with good accommodation was selected but the section was only a few days here when a move further forward was made.	
POIX-du-NORD	6-7.		Owing to the length of the advance moving out to no nearer to the V.E.S. was a eighty piece there.	
POIX-du-NORD — LOGBUIGNOL	7.		Section marched to LOGBUIGNOL north of the FOREST de MORMAL and slept there.	
LOGBUIGNOL — TETE NOIR	8.		Section marched to AULNOYE to-morning but the state of the roads, congestion of traffic also to the main route being blown up, it was decided that, just to night at TETE NOIR.	

Army Form C. 2118.

WAR DIARY
or
INTELLIGENCE SUMMARY.

29th Mobile Veterinary Section

November 1918

(Erase heading not required.)

Instructions regarding War Diaries and Intelligence Summaries are contained in F. S. Regs., Part II. and the Staff Manual respectively. Title pages will be prepared in manuscript.

Place	Date	Hour	Summary of Events and Information	Remarks and references to Appendices
TETE NOIR – HUNNOYE	9		Section proceeded across the SAMBRE and advanced to HUNNOYE. Motor lorries and disc harrows were put on as General Roadcart. A good billet for the men having found.	
HUNNOYE	9-12		Very little work was done while at HUNNOYE and fortunately so as to move back to the V.E.S. horses have been impracticable in the town.	
HUNNOYE VENDEGIES au BOIS	12		Owing to Armistice having been put in section marched with Division HQ to INCHY, halting the night at VENDEGIES-au-BOIS.	
VENDEGIES au BOIS – INCHY	13		Section resumed march to INCHY.	
INCHY	13-30		While at INCHY little work was done owing to the fact that the Mobile were a rest area attached to the Veterinary Evacuating Station as was all the sick stock there. With the great reduction in strength, one is able to make the condition of [illegible] of the men comfortable and the further [illegible]	

D. D. & L., London, E.C. (A300.) Wt. W2771/M298 730/00 5/17 Sch. 52 Forms C2118/14

WAR DIARY
or
INTELLIGENCE SUMMARY.

(Erase heading not required.)

Army Form C. 2118.

29th Mobile Veterinary Section
November 1918

Place	Date	Hour	Summary of Events and Information	Remarks and references to Appendices
INCH	13/5		Nothing known as before. Nothing to advance at times. Issued as PO & an Nos.D. BERTIMONT and All NO VE animals were registered whereupon the grooms in the many or company horses of the lot a/c to 6. The stamp of the animals being sent to sane kettering mobile F. to animals are retained and none disposed of. 9 Animals were retained and none disposed of. Train 86 Crossed Gabriel 70 were of this division. 10 were in care of 6 units and one cnr of G Division a had destroyed.	

P.P. [signature]
a/s 29 mobile let sector

WAR DIARY or INTELLIGENCE SUMMARY

Army Form C. 2118.

29 Motor Machine Gun Battery
December 1918

Place	Date	Hour	Summary of Events and Information	Remarks and references to Appendices
INCHY	1-8		At INCHY performing routine duty. No need for shoeing attention.	
INCHY & MASNIERES	8		Section marched with 50 INFANTRY BRIGADE group and in rear of the division to MASNIERES en route for the rest area near ABBEVILLE.	
MASNIERES – HERMIES	8-9		Continued march to HERMIES.	
HERMIES – MIRAUMONT	9-10		Continued march to MIRAUMONT.	
MIRAUMONT & ALBERT	10-11		Continued march to ALBERT.	
ALBERT – QUERRIEU	11-12		Continued march to QUERRIEU.	
QUERRIEU – PICQUIGNY	12-13		Continued march to PICQUIGNY.	

Army Form C. 2118.

WAR DIARY
or
INTELLIGENCE SUMMARY.
29 Mobile Veterinary Section
December 1916

(Erase heading not required.)

Place	Date	Hour	Summary of Events and Information	Remarks and references to Appendices
PICQUIGNY	13-14		Continued march to HALLENCOURT. Our first shot.	
HALLENCOURT			The march was a long and arduous one and carried out in most trying conditions, heavy rains and the fact the horses were employed in no part old and het, the kickets than got the staging over were considerably longer.	
HALLENCOURT	14-19		At HALLENCOURT owing to the want of accommodation for men horses I was directed to move the section to a better area situate near Oisemont. COCQUERIE a small village on the Somme near PONT REMY. here I unoccupied was selected. Guides were sent for to three horse lines going on at the Chateau and good sick horse lines gone on at the Chateau and good sick horse lines procured. COCQUERIE dirt advances from ABBEVILLE by rail 10 kilogs. the troubles have covered the post every convenient way.	
COCQUERIE	19-31		Animals were admitted and disposed of as follows 500 became 154 Animals were admitted. Sick 152 Animals have evacuated to Veterinary Hospital about 2 Animals were destroyed as incurable. N.G. Stewart Lt. RAVC	

Army Form C. 2118.

WAR DIARY
or
INTELLIGENCE SUMMARY.
(Erase heading not required.)

29 Mobile Veterinary Section
January 1919.

Place	Date	Hour	Summary of Events and Information	Remarks and references to Appendices
COCQUERIL	1-31.		Section at COCQUERIL during the whole of the month attending to ordinary section duty and the evacuation of the sick to ABBEVILLE, but no light or call for no special mention for this period. A number of the section horses being classed "Y" have been sent to the Base for reparation to England and in view of the demobilization of the chinese Army this is out so required the movement of these animals has not could for. Owing to outbreak of chronic Epizootic lymphangitis in No 5. VETERINARY EVACUATION STATION 120 Unit has ceased to function as the V.E.S.O. 28.1.19 from with the motor Ambulance brigade but no more animals as hitherto to be evacuated to ABBEVILLE 192 Animals are now admitted sick and disposed of. Evacuated 155 Returned to Units 23	

M Wright

WAR DIARY

INTELLIGENCE SUMMARY.

29th Mobile Veterinary Section
February 1919

Place	Date	Hour	Summary of Events and Information	Remarks and references to Appendices
Roguel	1st-28th		Section of Regiment during the whole of month's carrying out ordinary section duties, also functioning as M.V.S. evacuating sick animals to No 14 Vet Hospt at Abbeville. Capt Keppel D.C. Section promoted to D.A.D.V.S. 17th Div. & moved to D.H.Q. on 10th. Capt Allen R.D.V.C. in tempt command of Section from 11th to 26th. he being relieved by Nicholas — 275 sick animals were evacuated to the hospital and with 5.00 Z animals were passed through the section for use of Regmts	

WAR DIARY
INTELLIGENCE SUMMARY

Army Form C. 2118.

Place	Date	Hour	Summary of Events and Information	Remarks and references to Appendices
Bogoserru	19th Sept	3 pm	Sector at Bogoserru being much patrolled today. Two carrier outposts of V.F.S. were seen and fired on with Germans Levy and 16 New Native Recruits. Eight Natives wounded one and three of Sector Fathers. Pvt & Capt P.W. Hann & MC 2nd 1873 Reinforcements wounded to white hospital 202 " Gebel through Sector to Enemy Enemy Thought on the 27th old estimate two Coys M.E.P. and men severely defortigued prior to 14th S.L.S.	

www.ingramcontent.com/pod-product-compliance
Lightning Source LLC
Chambersburg PA
CBHW080904230426
43664CB00016B/2719